PRAISE FOR *DEC*

While other politicians make cheap points demoniz-ing people who use drugs, Kennedy Stewart courageously led and advocated for a compassionate, evidence-based approach to substance use. I hope his successful campaign to decriminalize drugs is a historic starting point in emerging from the costly, ineffective and deadly war on drugs.

— **Benjamin Perrin**, UBC law professor and author of *Overdose: Heartbreak and Hope in Canada's Opioid Crisis*

It's hard to believe that just twenty years ago the idea of decrim-inalization of drugs was a non-starter. Kennedy Stewart's clear leadership and advocacy at all levels of government showed that we can save lives and end the assault on people who use drugs. A humane and rights-based approach is possible.

— **Libby Davies**, member of Parliament, Vancouver East, 1997–2015

When many politicians were moving back to the "War on Drugs" mentality, Kennedy Stewart was looking for solutions that could help all citizens in Vancouver. Before even being elected he reached out to me and other health advocates in the Downtown Eastside to see how we could build a coalition. That thinking is what has allowed the City of Vancouver to continue to lead on the illicit drug issue.

— **Dean Wilson**, peer facilitation lead, British Columbia Centre on Substance Use

Kennedy Stewart used his platform in politics to end pro-hibition and advance a public health approach to the opioid crisis. In the face of a devastating challenge to his community and country, he showed leadership with his work to follow the evidence to save lives.

— **Nathaniel Erskine-Smith**, member of Parliament, Beaches–East York

DECRIM

KENNEDY STEWART

DECRIM

How We Decriminalized Drugs in British Columbia

**HARBOUR
PUBLISHING**

Harbour Publishing Co. Ltd.
P.O. Box 219, Madeira Park, BC, VON 2HO
www.harbourpublishing.com

Edited by Brian Lynch
Indexed by Colleen Bidner
Cover design by Dwayne Dobson
Text design by Libris Simas Ferraz / Onça Publishing
Printed and bound in Canada
Printed on 100% recycled paper

 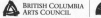

Harbour Publishing acknowledges the support of the Canada Council for the
Arts, the Government of Canada, and the Province of British Columbia through
the BC Arts Council.

Library and Archives Canada Cataloguing in Publication
Title: Decrim : how we decriminalized drugs in British Columbia / Kennedy
    Stewart.
Names: Stewart, Kennedy, author.
Identifiers: Canadiana (print) 20220494541 | Canadiana (ebook) 20220494592 |
    ISBN 9781990776304 (softcover) | ISBN 9781990776311 (EPUB)
Subjects: LCSH: Drug legalization—British Columbia. | LCSH: Drug legalization—
    Social aspects—British Columbia. | LCSH: Narcotic laws—British
    Columbia. | LCSH: Drug abuse—British Columbia. | LCSH: Drug abuse—
    Social aspects—British Columbia.
Classification: LCC HV5840.C32 B757 2023 | DDC 362.2909711—dc23

To my mom, Cathy Stewart,
from whom all my values flow.

CONTENTS

PREFACE

READERS WHO WANT TO KNOW HOW DRUGS CAME TO BE decriminalized in Vancouver, British Columbia, Canada, should know I have no experience in many important areas related to this topic. I do not use controlled or illegal drugs and have no direct experience with injecting or inhaling heroin, cocaine or other illicit substances. I am not a front-line peer worker, firefighter, paramedic, nurse or doctor, and have never revived someone who has overdosed or provided care to them afterwards. I have never attended a drug policy reform protest. I am not a police officer and have never had to interpret, stop or solve a crime. I am not a health policy researcher and have never received a grant or published studies on illicit drug use.

Instead, the insights I provide on this topic come from my experience as an insider politician willing to explain how we realized a significant, and unlikely, reform in one of the most taboo areas of public policy. I was never privy to the inner workings of the federal cabinet while serving as a Canadian

New Democratic Party (NDP) member of Parliament (MP), but in serving for seven years on the opposition benches I developed a deep understanding of how national politics works. I also spent four years as one of the most left-leaning (or "liberal," in the United States of America) politicians ever to serve as mayor of Vancouver, elected to office mere months after being arrested for blockading a new oil pipeline planned to run through the unceded territories of many First Nations. As mayor, I had an all-access backstage pass to everything affecting Vancouver, including the efforts to combat illicit drug–related deaths. I made key decisions on the city's decriminalization efforts and had many private discussions with other critical decision-makers, including Canadian prime minister Justin Trudeau, British Columbia premiers John Horgan and David Eby, Canadian federal health ministers Patty Hajdu and Jean-Yves Duclos, Canadian federal minister for mental health and addictions Carolyn Bennett, and BC ministers of mental health and addictions Judy Darcy and Sheila Malcolmson. It is from this perspective I write this book with the hope that any lessons I can pass along will help others seeking to make progressive political change in the communities they love.

There are thousands of media stories describing the horrors of drug use and hope for a better future for those affected. There are hundreds of valuable academic papers outlining which policy solutions are most effective. This book takes neither a purely journalistic nor a purely academic approach. It contains stories, but few interviews. It contains data, but they are not plugged in to complicated statistical formulas. Instead, this book combines a bit of both approaches in hoping to be of use to all. A note of caution: this book may be triggering as it discusses details of how people who use drugs (drug users from here on) live and die and how families cope, and as it frequently refers to Canada's Indigenous Genocide, poverty and homelessness.

This book tells the story of decriminalization from my own perspective. Chapter 1 provides an overview as to how drug policy generally changes. Chapter 2 offers context about the city of Vancouver and describes key political structures and actors. Chapter 3 explores the tragedy of illicit drug-related deaths in Vancouver and significant local drug policy reform efforts prior to decriminalization. Chapter 4 outlines how decriminalization emerged as a leading policy reform idea and describes my encounters with other drug policy reform attempts, including cannabis legalization, while serving as a Canadian member of Parliament between 2011 and 2018. Chapter 5 explains my journey to being elected the fortieth mayor of Vancouver with a mandate to address the illicit drug-related death crisis as well as the obstacles blocking reform—including Prime Minister Justin Trudeau's and Premier John Horgan's opposition to decriminalization. Chapter 6 tells how the COVID-19 pandemic made the illicit drug-related death crisis so much worse, and how Prime Minister Trudeau's decision to appoint Liberal MP Patty Hajdu as minister of health proved a watershed moment in the process by which drugs were decriminalized in British Columbia. Chapter 7 explains how our decriminalization efforts withered and almost died on the vine, and Chapter 8 describes how the window for change was once again thrown open. Chapter 9 outlines how the problem, policy and politics came together to make decriminalization a reality. I talk about the aftermath of the federal government's decision to approve British Columbia's decriminalization application, including my election loss, in Chapter 10. Finally, in Chapter 11, I offer ideas about where to go from here by exploring what could have been done to save my own family member, Susan Havelock, from dying from poisoned drugs.

This book seeks to convey two general lessons. First, policy change is extremely difficult to achieve. Substantively altering the current course of any government comes only after years of frustrating activism when advocates endure failure after disappointing failure, often with the knowledge that whatever new direction a government eventually decides to pursue will never be enough. Second, policy change is extremely risky for those who try to make it happen, people I call "change agents." Voters tend to cling to the status quo and punish officials who rock their boats. Take it from me, the now ex-mayor of Vancouver. I feel it was worth losing my job to secure decriminalization and other important anti-poverty investments, as it will go at least some way to improving the lives of our worst-suffering neighbours and take us another step down the path of ending the war on drug users. In combination, these two lessons suggest that policy change is possible and often comes with a steep price, but I believe it is the only way forward.

1

HOW DRUG POLICY CHANGES

WEEK AFTER WEEK, EMAILS LANDED IN MY MAYOR'S OFFICE inbox telling me how many people had died from what staff describe as a "drug overdose" in Vancouver during the previous seven days.[1] Fourteen, ten, two, five, twelve... Although the subject line was "Weekly overdose data," what was really being counted is better called "illicit drug–related deaths." This is an important distinction, as regular drug users know which drugs they need, how much to take, how to take them, and what to do in the case of an overdose. But in an era where fentanyl and other potent substances are so prevalent and inexpertly mixed with other illicit drugs, there is really no way for drug users to tell what they are injecting or inhaling. No matter how experienced, drug users can no longer accurately predict how unexpected combinations of drugs will impact them, a situation that often leads to an overdose where a person's breathing and heart rate slow, oxygen stops properly flowing to the brain, foam forms in the mouth, and, in too many cases, the person suffers permanent injury or death.

Although it goes against the dominant narrative, which sometimes feels like it comes from the film *Reefer Madness*, most drug users live productive lives if they can accurately assess and safely access what they need to put into their bodies. Also counter to this harmful narrative, ready access to safer drugs appears to be the only way forward for those suffering with substance use disorder (defined by the us-based National Institute of Mental Health as "a treatable mental disorder that affects a person's brain and behavior, leading to their inability to control their use of substances").[2] However, treatment is not often readily available, and what is offered often does not work for the vast majority of drug users, who then relapse.

I was aware of the illicit drug–related death crisis well before being elected mayor in 2018, but it was only during the municipal election campaign that I really began to realize the full horror facing our city, after speaking with activists and committed health-care professionals in Vancouver's Downtown Eastside neighbourhood. I also met many peer-responders and firefighters working every day to bring victims back from the dead, time and time again, frustrated by the lack of urgency in their national parliament, provincial legislature and city hall. Perhaps the hardest conversations were with those who had lost loved ones, including, eventually, members of my own family. These and other encounters transformed my understanding of what was really happening in Vancouver from an abstract issue without a face to a very real tragedy.

On October 20, 2018, I was elected the first independent mayor of Vancouver in thirty years by under a thousand votes. If you asked me on election night, I would have told you that significant drug policy reform in Vancouver was impossible. There were huge barriers to change, despite the obvious need and a well-organized and sophisticated drug-user activist community. Not only was the council over which I presided deeply fractured, with no governing experience, but it also had little formal authority to take independent action on public health issues. As will be later explained in detail, while senior governments have the power to make change, national and provincial cabinet members are often opposed to making bold moves on controlled or illegal drug policy, or even discussing the topic in any real way. Finally, what I did not know in 2018 was that any potential drug policy change would be made during the COVID-19 pandemic—the worst crisis ever to hit Vancouver.

And yet, despite these obstacles, on January 31, 2023, Vancouver became the first major city in Canada to decriminalize drugs, meaning it is no longer a criminal offence to possess small amounts of certain illicit drugs. This revolutionary change occurred when a federal exemption to the national Controlled Drugs and Substances Act took effect, province-wide, in British Columbia. Under the exemption, adults aged eighteen years and older will no longer be arrested or charged for possessing opioids, cocaine, methamphetamine or MDMA for personal use, up to a combined total of 2.5 grams. Decriminalization changes how we police drug use in BC by restricting the ability of law enforcement officials to interact with drug users, arrest them or seize their drugs. Although the terms are often confused, drug decriminalization differs from drug legalization or "safer supply." A drug is "decriminalized" when governments remove criminal sanctions for its use, but deems it illegal to produce, deal or sell. Governments "legalize" a drug when they permit its use and sale under certain licensing conditions by government or private vendors. "Safer supply" is when governments provide a regulated supply of drugs, often free of charge, as a substitute for drugs traditionally available only through the illicit market.

It makes sense that the seeds of decriminalization sprouted in Vancouver. This city has long been at the forefront of drug policy reform. But drug decriminalization is different from, say, opening the country's first authorized needle exchange program. The needle exchange program was hugely important and created a new type of facility that was later replicated in other locations. Decriminalization affects an entire regulatory framework, more closely resembling cannabis legalization than, say, the opening of a supervised consumption site. While different in nature, all these innovations are big, unlikely policy changes. All are worth better understanding.

Throughout history, humans have created codes and rules rewarding and punishing different types of behaviour, and empowering certain community members to enforce these regulations. This book is based on the simple initial assumption that the status quo for any policy issue is very difficult to change, as it is so entrenched in our laws, institutions and culture. Opportunities for policy change occur when problems within the community emerge or worsen, consensus begins to form around solutions to these policy problems, and people with different energies enter the political arena. But even simultaneous variations in these three conditions—problem, policy and politics—do not guarantee that governments will change course.[3]

Governments only ever address very few of the myriad possible *problems* facing their communities, including everything from keeping kids busy after school to avoiding nuclear war. Governments begin to pay attention to a particular problem when regular monitoring—for example, through inflation statistics—shows a significant variation in the status quo, or when a sudden event, such as a mass shooting, prompts public outcry. But "paying attention" does not automatically mean "changing policy," as the latter requires additional and simultaneous factors to occur.

One of these additional factors is agreement as to what new *policy* the government should implement. But arriving at this agreement is extremely difficult, as lobbyists, civil servants, academics and affected community members generate a massive range of possible policy solutions—each with its own pitfalls. Lobbyists may advocate attractive policy solutions, but only those benefiting their employers. Civil servants often devise elegant, but expensive or politically risky, proposals. Academics may have great theoretical, but ultimately impractical, ideas about what to do. Citizen groups may push for local improvements but fail to balance the needs of the wider community. Change is not guaranteed even when consensus begins to emerge around how to best address a particular problem.

Those holding *political* power tend to support the status quo, as that is what got them into power in the first place, and they know change can be unpopular and risky. However, agendas can change when different people are elected to fill decision-making positions. Or—and this is important to the decriminalization story—sitting politicians change their minds and decide to do something different. Even so, electing different politicians or having some change their minds does not guarantee policy change.

On rare occasions, worsening problems, policy consensus and the emergence of reform-minded politicians collide and open windows of opportunity through which reformers can drive policy. Like surfers waiting for a big wave, policy reformers lie in wait for a chance to secure policy change for their own satisfaction or on behalf of a particular community. Some fail to secure change, some succeed. Some live to fight another day, some perish on the policy battlefield.

All reformers agree that decriminalization will only go so far in reducing illicit drug–related deaths, and that it is not a panacea. But we all must remember that reducing illicit drug–related deaths is just one important objective of drug policy reform. We all need to heed my friend and renowned activist Karen Ward, who says it is not good enough to settle for drug users just being "not dead." We need to enact policies and laws to ensure their lives are as rich and joyous as possible. Decriminalization will save lives and take us one step farther along the path to ending the destructive war on drug users. Thus, while I know decriminalization is a sign of progress, I also know that the weekly overdose-death emails to the mayor's office will likely continue, and too many of our neighbours, family members and friends will needlessly die torturous deaths. Much more needs to be done. Fourteen, ten, two, five, twelve...

2

HEAVEN AND HELL IN VANCOUVER

VANCOUVER IS A CITY OF EXTREMES. MOUNTAINOUS AND coastal. Ancient and modern. Dense and sprawling. Decadent and impoverished. Multicultural and genocidal. These extremes play out in neighbourhoods where people live both the longest and shortest lives in the country. Where young people flock to explore their high-tech dreams and where too many die from toxic drugs. Three-quarters of the population have post-secondary education but largely ignore the science surrounding one of Canada's greatest health policy disasters.

Welcome to Vancouver

Vancouver is a thriving port city nestled between the rugged Coast Mountain Range and the Pacific Ocean. With nearly 700,000 residents, the City of Vancouver is the core of the larger Metro Vancouver region of approximately 2.5 million people. It is a rich city, with 30 percent of all households reporting annual incomes of over $100,000. It is an expensive city, with the average home worth well over $1 million.[4] It is a diverse city. Over half of the residents are of minority ancestry, and the city is home to a large and active Two-Spirit, Lesbian, Gay, Bisexual, Transgender, Queer, Questioning, Intersex, Asexual, Pansexual, Agender, Gender Queer, Bigender, Gender Variant, Pangender (2SLGBTQIA+) community. Vancouver has a very low homicide rate compared with other North American cities, with 2.7 murders per 100,000 residents in 2021.

Digging even slightly below the surface reveals extremely challenging big-city problems Vancouverites are often reluctant to acknowledge. For one, most of British Columbia, including Vancouver, is situated on land stolen by the British colonial government prior to Canada's 1867 Confederation. No formal treaties were signed between the British Crown and the three Indigenous First Nations on whose lands Vancouver currently rests—the xʷməθkʷəy̓əm (Musqueam), Sḵwx̱wú7mesh Úxwumixw (Squamish) and səl̓ilw̓ətaʔɬ (Tsleil-Waututh). The original inhabitants in what we now call Vancouver were driven off their ancestral territory. They were also confined to tiny reserves and subjected to what the Canadian Parliament recently declared as "genocidal practices," including being denied basic human rights and abominable abuse at state-sponsored residential schools.[5]

Tragically, Canada's Indigenous Genocide plays itself out on Vancouver's streets. Approximately 40 percent of the over two thousand people identified in 2020 as living without permanent homes have Indigenous ancestry, despite making up only 2 percent of the population.[6] Extreme poverty and intergenerational trauma have created conditions where as many as four thousand Indigenous women and girls have gone missing or been murdered over the past thirty years in Canada, including, horrifically, those murdered by a Vancouver-based serial killer.[7] Many settlers (non-Indigenous people) also suffer. Over 20 percent of Vancouver's population lives below the poverty line, despite, for example, federal, provincial and local governments working together to provide more social and low-cost housing per capita than any other municipality in British Columbia.[8]

This type of trauma often results in drug use, which is becoming increasingly fatal owing to toxic drugs flooding the system. The British Columbia Coroners Service reported 2,314 illicit drug–related deaths in 2022. This equates to 44 deaths per 100,000 residents, or over six preventable deaths per day. As shown in Figure 1, illicit drug–related death is the fourth-leading cause of mortality in the province, behind cancer, heart disease and Alzheimer's disease. It is also the second leading cause of death in terms of years of life lost and the leading cause of death among young people, with the average age of death being 44 years.[9] According to Angus Reid survey data, 11 percent of British Columbians, almost 400,000 adult residents, say they know someone who has died from an opioid overdose.[10] This phenomenon is centred in BC but is spreading across Canada. In 2021, 7,993 people died from what Health Canada calls "opioid harm-related deaths."[11] This equates to twenty-one deaths per 100,000 residents, or approximately twenty-six preventable deaths per day nationwide. Angus Reid reports that 5 percent of Canadians, about 1.5 million residents, have known someone who died from an overdose.[12]

This extremely high rate of death happens everywhere in Vancouver, all over the city, in every neighbourhood. Recently, I went to my favourite local restaurant with my brother, Evan. A friend we have known for decades, whom I'll call Shayne, stopped by to say hello, then told us how he had lost his friend to poisoned cocaine, most likely laced with fentanyl, the previous week. Shayne hadn't seen his friend for a few days, nor had his work colleagues. The missing friend was a good guy and diligent worker, and people grew worried. Shayne called his friend's landlord to check on his friend, but there was no answer even after hard knocks on his door. The landlord reviewed security camera footage and saw the friend go into the building, but never leave. Shayne eventually convinced the landlord to let him into his friend's apartment. He found his friend dead in bed with a video game controller locked in his rigor mortis–stricken hands. He stayed with him until the paramedics arrived to take him to the morgue.

The horror of this experience was obvious on Shayne's face as he told us his story. Unfortunately, the conversation didn't end there. After listening to Shayne, another friend at the table, whom I'll call Gary, told us about a friend of his who too had just died from tainted cocaine. Gary's friend had taken the drug, climbed on her regular bus, and died on the way home. If that wasn't tragic enough, she was not discovered for hours, after going around and around the route because the driver thought she was just sleeping and was

Figure 1. Top 10 causes of death in British Columbia (January to December 2022)

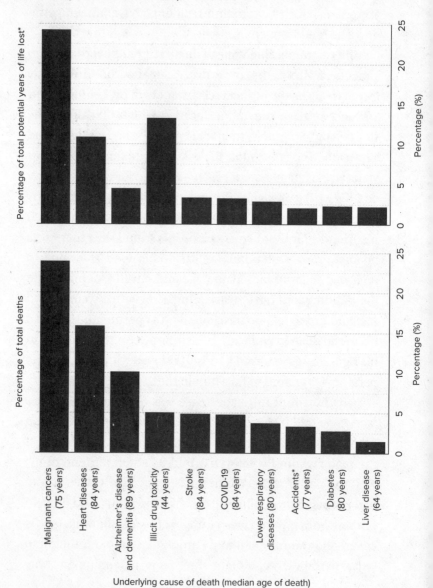

Source: British Columbia Centre for Disease Control, "Top 15 Causes of Death (Ranking) in BC for 2022."

kind enough not to wake her. At the same table, my brother pulled out his phone and showed me a picture of his friend who had recently died from poisoned drugs as well.

That is just one casual conversation between friends on a regular afternoon, but stories like these are everywhere. Those affecting middle-class folks tend to make the media, but, sadly, they are much more prevalent in lower-income areas. Personally, I've had the unnerving privilege of having many conversations with the true heroes of this government policy–driven catastrophe, the peers who work at authorized and unauthorized overdose prevention sites. These under-paid front-line workers revive dozens and dozens of friends and neighbours while losing others. I have met firefighters from Vancouver Fire and Rescue Hall No. 2 in the Downtown Eastside, on medical leave after reviving a patient multiple times on multiple days only to have that same person die during an attempted resuscitation later that week. It is hard to believe we are letting one of the most beautiful cities in the world be a living hell for so many: drug users, their families and friends, and those providing health-care services.

Instead of running away from this issue, we need to get real about the prevalence of drug use. The 2019 Canadian Alcohol and Drugs Survey indicates nearly 18 percent of Canadians (approximately seven million people) report using illegal drugs in their lifetime, with 5 percent (approximately two million) using within the previous year.[13] When applied to Vancouver, these estimates suggest that upwards of 125,000 of Vancouver's 700,000 residents have used controlled or illicit drugs in their lifetime, with nearly 35,000 doing so in the last year, and perhaps as many as 10,000 to 15,000 living with a substance use disorder. We need to get real about the risk of dying of toxic drugs: one person a day here in the city of Vancouver, six people per day in the province of British Columbia, twenty-six people per day in Canada dying alone while playing video games in bed or riding the bus home. We need to realize that the current approach to saving lives is not working, nor are the Band-Aid solutions we are using to stem illicit drug–related overdose deaths.

Governance

It is worth understanding a bit more about who makes decisions in Canada's eighth-largest municipality, as Vancouver is the epicentre of the country's illicit drug–related death crisis and the wellspring of past drug policy innovation. I could not point you to any city government in the world with less formal authority over the geographic area that it is supposed to govern than Vancouver's municipal government. This lack of local authority is in part due to Canada's federal system of government, and partly because Canadian provinces have been reluctant to delegate too much of their constitutional authority to municipalities.

Starting at the national level, powers afforded to the federal government under Section 91 of the Constitution Act, 1867, deeply affect Vancouver and every other Canadian city. These federal powers include jurisdictional authority over taxation, immigration and countless other areas that impact the day-to-day lives of Canadians. While the federal government rarely directly intervenes in individual municipalities, their general powers can have great local impact. For example, as will be discussed at length later, the Controlled Drugs and Substances Act (CDSA) sets the framework for the control of all drugs in Canada. Overseen by the Canadian federal minister of health, the CDSA bans all drugs other than those specifically allowed through prescription or. ministerial exemption. The 2018 decision to legalize cannabis in Canada, for example, was exclusively a federal government decision that impacted all Canadian municipalities, which had to change local policy and bylaws to license pot shops.

Section 92 of the Constitution Act, 1867, recognizes that the structure and authority of all municipal governments in Canada are the sole domain of provincial and territorial governments. As "creatures of the province," municipalities are created, amalgamated or abolished by a simple legislative act, with the same act usually delineating the scope of local government authority. Successive British Columbian provincial governments have chosen to make their municipal governments some of the weakest on the planet when it comes to the areas of policy over which provinces and territories have authority, including health policy.

The City of Vancouver was created by the Province of British Columbia through provincial statute in 1886 and expanded through amalgamation before its current boundaries and 115-square-kilometre land area was established in 1929. The responsibilities and authority of the Vancouver mayor and ten city councillors are set out in the Vancouver Charter, with the most consequential being land-use planning and property-tax collection to fund core services like policing, fire protection and infrastructure maintenance. The main sources of revenue are property taxes and user fees, as local governments in British Columbia do not have the ability to charge income tax or sales tax, nor are they provided with significant senior government grants. Canadian municipalities cannot run operating deficits or exceed provincially determined debt levels.

Vancouver also has an elected board of parks and recreation, as established in the Vancouver Charter, and an elected school board, governed by the School Act, to respectively oversee leisure and educational services with authority over everything from swimming pools to school budgets. Policing in Vancouver is funded through municipal property taxes, but as prescribed by the provincial Police Act, law enforcement service provision is also outside the purview of Vancouver city council and rests with a board of directors appointed by the Province of British Columbia. The board sets broad policing policy and directly employs the police executive and front-line officers, with the chief constable having sole responsibility for policing operations. While the mayor of Vancouver chairs the police board, the mayor cannot move or vote on motions. A recent ruling by the British Columbia provincial government now means municipal governments cannot refuse police board funding requests, no matter what the circumstances.

The City of Vancouver is one of twenty-three local government bodies (including one Treaty First Nation—the Tsawwassen First Nation) making up the Greater Vancouver Regional District, more commonly known as Metro Vancouver. As set out in the Local Government Act, locally elected mayors, councillors and Tsawwassen First Nation representatives sit as Metro Vancouver directors to negotiate and make policy about sewage, water, solid waste and other infrastructure-related issues. The South Coast British Columbia Transportation Authority Act provides TransLink—the organization responsible for public transportation (buses, trains and ferries) in the city of Vancouver and municipalities in the surrounding Metro area—with the authority over transit planning and operations, with decisions made by a board of directors as well as the Mayors' Council on Regional Transportation. The twenty-three-member Mayors' Council is responsible for approving fares and long-term planning, while a board of directors composed of seven individuals appointed by the Mayors' Council, the Mayors' Council chair and vice-chair, and up to two members appointed by the Province oversee day-to-day transit operations through a board-appointed chief executive officer.

Finally, public health is also under the exclusive constitutional jurisdiction of the Province, which delegates policy and service provision authority to appointed regional health boards, not municipalities. The city of Vancouver is in the Vancouver Coastal Health service area, with VCH delivering community, hospital and long-term care services to more than one million people in communities including Vancouver, Richmond and North Shore, as well as coastal municipalities. VCH overdose outreach teams work with the Vancouver fire department and emergency health services to get clients access to acute and community services, operate overdose prevention sites and deliver safer-supply initiatives.

Local Politics

Vancouver city council is composed of a mayor and ten councillors, as established under the Vancouver Charter. Vancouver has a "weak mayor system," as opposed to the "strong mayor system" found in other North American cities, such as New York. In New York, the mayor directly appoints deputy mayors and heads of agencies to execute policy decisions. The mayor of New York also sets the agenda for the City and its finances, on which council then votes. In Vancouver's weak mayor system, the mayor is just one of eleven council votes. All appointments, such as the city manager and fire chief, are approved by the whole of council, and any council member can place items on the council agenda or offer amendments from the floor, including during the budget process. When coupled with the limited range of powers afforded to council outlined in the last section, Vancouver's system might be best called a weak, weak mayor system.

Unlike all other major Canadian cities outside British Columbia, all elected Vancouver city council positions are gained through "at-large" elections. National, provincial and most municipal elections in Canada are conducted under single-member plurality, or first-past-the-post, systems where the community is divided into districts with one member elected per district. Under Vancouver's at-large electoral system, the city is not divided into smaller districts, but rather all ten council members are elected by the entire city using a first-ten-past-the-post system. Also, unlike in most Canadian cities, Vancouver politics has been dominated by local political parties since the 1930s. These include the once-dominant centre-right Non-Partisan Association (NPA), the venerable far-left Coalition of Progressive Electors (COPE), and the now defunct centrist Electors' Action Movement (TEAM), as well as more recently formed parties, such as the centrist Vision Vancouver, centrist Green Party of Vancouver, and centre-left OneCity, and new elector organizations, such as centre-right A Better City (ABC) and centre-left Forward Together.

The combination of at-large elections and numerous local political parties produces extremely skewed election results. For example, in the 1996 civic election the Non-Partisan Association took all ten (100 percent) of the council seats despite gaining just 50 percent of the available votes. In 2022, ABC ran seven of a possible ten council candidates, all of which were elected for ABC to secure 70 percent of council seats, despite winning just 35 percent of the total votes cast for council. In political science–speak, Vancouver's partisan, at-large electoral system is massively disproportional, where the first-place party is grossly overrewarded. At-large electoral systems have been demonstrated to discriminate against minority groups, and, as such, have been struck down by courts in many US cities.

I am very familiar with local elections in Vancouver, as I wrote my master's thesis in political science on this topic at Simon Fraser University in 1995. Supervised by Professor Paddy Smith, I traced every Vancouver municipal election since the city was incorporated in 1886, concluding that the at-large system ensures voters from Vancouver's wealthy West Side control who runs city hall. My work set me on a practical path to understanding local Vancouver politics, starting when local New Democratic Party member of Parliament Libby Davies asked me to present my thesis findings to a group of local activists shortly after I graduated, then quickly talked me into organizing for the Coalition of Progressive Electors during the 1996 civic election. The at-large system worked its magic in 1996, and COPE mayoral candidate Carmela Allevato and every single candidate who ran with her party lost to newly elected Mayor Philip Owen's Non-Partisan Association, which won twenty-seven of twenty-seven available council, park board and school board seats.

Vancouver voters are split into five groups: a large left, a large right, and a smaller middle, with very small far-left and far-right fringe groups. The key to victory for most Vancouver mayors is to ignore the fringe, secure support from either all left voters or all right voters, and then win enough votes from the centre to secure a majority. Most post-war Vancouver civic elections featured one main mayoral candidate from the left competing against one centre-right mayoral candidate. Left mayoral candidates always lost, as they secured support only from the left voter group, while centre-right mayoral candidates secured support from centre and right voters. This trend continued until 1972, when centre-left mayoral candidates emerged to challenge centre-right mayoral candidates and power shifted back and forth between the two candidate types. Since 1972, centre-left mayors have included Art Phillips (TEAM), Mike Harcourt (Independent), Larry Campbell (COPE) and Gregor Robertson (Vision Vancouver). Centre-right mayors have included Gordon Campbell (NPA), Philip Owen (NPA), Sam Sullivan (NPA) and Ken Sim (ABC).

As will be explained in later chapters, I am a left, as opposed to centre-left, politician and, as such, my 2018 election represents a break in the regular pattern of Vancouver voters electing either centre-left or centre-right mayors.

Vancouver looks beautiful in pictures, but those on the margins often live with huge challenges that average residents cannot even imagine. The level of suffering and death due to illicit drugs in a place that is seen by many as one of the best in the world in which to live is hard to understand. That governments seem unwilling to radically challenge the status quo and implement policies to save lives is even harder to comprehend. A good place to start to understand these barriers is to consider the formal rules determining who does what on the policy stage. In terms of drug policy, Vancouver city council has no authority over health policy or policing, and should, at least on paper, really have very little to do with moving forward measures to reduce illicit drug–related deaths, as these are provincial and federal government responsibilities. However, municipal councils are elected by residents who do not have the time or desire to read constitutions and legislative acts, and so expect their mayor and council to address problems in their city, even when council does not have the formal authority to do so. This is especially the case when provincial and federal governments do what they can to avoid long-standing or emerging issues, such as those connected with mental health and addiction. As we'll explore in the next chapter, Vancouver city councils have a long history of stepping outside their formal authority to address these issues.

3

THE DESPERATE STRUGGLE FOR DRUG POLICY REFORM

D RUG POLICY INNOVATION FORMS AN IMPORTANT PART OF Vancouver's global identity, as for sixty-five years we have developed innovative solutions to help save lives. Recent examples of drug policy innovation help explain how illicit drugs came to be decriminalized in 2023, including how Vancouver became the first city in Canada to open an authorized needle exchange program in 1989, and how, in 2003, North America's first supervised consumption site—Insite—was approved to open in Vancouver. The needle exchange program and supervised consumption site came into being when drug users organized within their community to save lives, often breaking the law to do so. These efforts quickly gained support from local health-care professionals and, with the two groups now working together, were able to secure local, provincial and federal support. Municipal politicians, who are typically much more immediately accessible to grassroots drug-policy reform advocates, are often the first to act and do what they can according to their formal authority, while pushing the provincial and federal governments to step up and tackle problems for which they are ultimately responsible. Provincial and federal governments are usually reluctant to initiate drug policy innovation, leaving it to local actors to lead the change, with senior governments sometimes later adopting and scaling up these locally generated reforms.

Illicit Drug–Related Deaths in Vancouver

Drugs have always killed people in Vancouver. For years, legal alcohol was the most common cause of drug-related death, as people died from asphyxiation, allergic reactions, driving while impaired or organ failure. Society treats booze differently than controlled and illicit drugs, even though the former is routinely more devastating to families and communities. Not only is there less stigma attached to drinking than to, say, heroin use, but the former is often seen and promoted as a positive activity you do to fit in and be part of the community, while the latter is viewed as deviant behaviour. It is very strange when you think about it for a couple of minutes.

Alcoholism has played a big role in my life. My mother often tells stories of uncles who struggled with drinking after serving on the front lines in world wars, while family members affected by their violence joined temperance movements. My dad, Keith, was an alcoholic, and his disease played a large role in him losing his job, our family going bankrupt, losing our home and falling into poverty. We never really got answers about the full extent of my father's alcoholism, as he moved away and cut off almost all communication with us in his sixties. We did not find out he had died until we were coincidentally informed by his former work colleague days after the fact. Painfully, he included no mention of any of us in his self-authored obituary.

My parents' bankruptcy was life-altering for me. I went from being a carefree twelve-year-old who took tennis lessons, rode his bike and went on nice middle-class vacations to being a scared little kid often charged with looking after my nine-year-old brother, Evan, and seven-year-old sister, Julia, as my mom, Cathy, worked non-stop to support us in a terrifying new environment. We went from living in a grand nineteenth-century mansion, now the historic Blomidon Inn, in the university town of Wolfville, Nova Scotia, to a hand-built, barely winterized log cabin on the remote South Mountain in the Annapolis Valley, where we drew water from Lumsden Pond. The South Mountain was known for intergenerational poverty, bootlegging and incest rings. It is where I developed an instinct to survive and my permanent class consciousness.

Drinking is a huge part of East Coast culture. From the age of fifteen, I played rock music in bars in bands that challenged audiences to outdrink us. Too many of us drank too much, often to deal with unresolved trauma. It was not uncommon to see big parties, drunk students and car wrecks on any given weekend. Many could not stop. I relied on alcohol as a crutch, binge-drinking a dozen beers or shots multiple times a week. I drank until I was sick or blacked out on many, many occasions. This behaviour was a required component of fitting in where I grew up, but, weirdly, other drugs were taboo. We were constantly warned of the dangers of marijuana, and while I took LSD once, I have never tried anything harder. Just say no to drugs—now drink up!

Vancouver was like Nova Scotia when I moved to the West Coast in the late 1980s on a one-way ticket and $100 my grandmother had given me. I was around the party culture as I played in the award-winning pop-rock band State of Mind throughout my early twenties. There was more emphasis on weed and less on booze in Vancouver. While there was some heroin and cocaine in my circles, it was mostly soft drugs and booze. I never saw people injecting and rarely saw them snort anything. But things began to change as harder drugs started to flood the city and drug users began to die at an unbelievable rate that even uninformed bassists like me noticed, starting in the early 1990s.

The gruesome line in Figure 2 demonstrates the number of people per 100,000 living in Vancouver who have suffered an illicit drug–related death, starting in 1986, when local health officials began reporting these statistics. Deaths solely due to alcohol are not included, as booze is legal, although alcohol is often reported as also being in the person's system when they die from illicit drugs. Regular controlled and illicit drug users know from whom to buy their drugs, how to use them, how much to take and how to deal with the effects. Thus, illicit drug deaths generally occur because drug users accidentally overdose by taking too much of one drug, taking some fatal combination of drugs, or believing they are taking one thing when they are really taking something else.

Early statistics indicate that illicit drug–related deaths were rare, with about twenty deaths per year in the city of

Figure 2. Annual illicit drug–related deaths per 100,000, City of Vancouver (1986–2022)

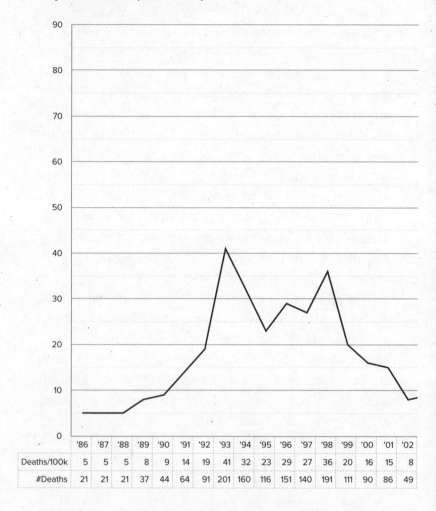

	'86	'87	'88	'89	'90	'91	'92	'93	'94	'95	'96	'97	'98	'99	'00	'01	'02
Deaths/100k	5	5	5	8	9	14	19	41	32	23	29	27	36	20	16	15	8
#Deaths	21	21	21	37	44	64	91	201	160	116	151	140	191	111	90	86	49

Source: British Columbia Coroners Service, "Statistical Reports on Deaths in British Columbia," and Office of the Chief Coroner, *Report of the Task Force into Illicit Narcotic Overdose Deaths in British Columbia,* 1994.

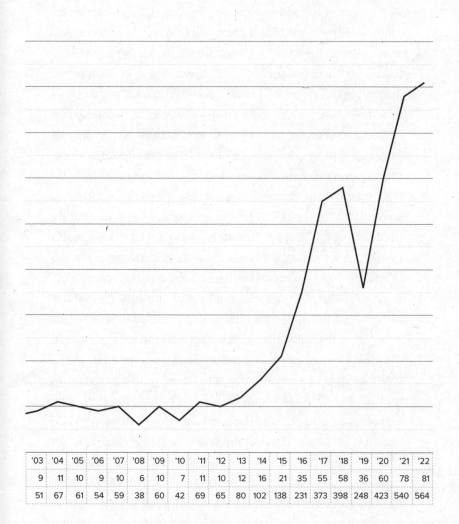

'03	'04	'05	'06	'07	'08	'09	'10	'11	'12	'13	'14	'15	'16	'17	'18	'19	'20	'21	'22
9	11	10	9	10	6	10	7	11	10	12	16	21	35	55	58	36	60	78	81
51	67	61	54	59	38	60	42	69	65	80	102	138	231	373	398	248	423	540	564

Vancouver in the 1980s. Coroner reports show these deaths often occurred when illicit drugs, such as heroin and cocaine, were mixed with alcohol. Things began to change in the early 1990s, when drug-related deaths exploded in Vancouver. According to former BC Chief Coroner Vince Cain, this spike was not due to an increase in the number of people using heroin and cocaine, but rather to inadvertent deaths caused by an unusually pure supply of these drugs suddenly flooding the market. Experienced drug users thought they were taking heroin or cocaine of a certain potency, but instead were injecting, smoking, snorting or swallowing something much, much stronger. The increased rate of drug-related deaths began to decline in 1998 and stabilized after 2002.

Illicit drug–related deaths in Vancouver became constant over the next decade at a rate of about 10 deaths per 100,000 residents. The number of drug-related deaths began to increase dramatically in 2012, exploding to reach a high of 564 deaths in 2022, or 81 deaths per 100,000 people. These types of deaths are now the fifth most frequent cause of mortality in British Columbia, behind cancer, heart disease, Alzheimer's and stroke. The median age of those who die is forty-four years, making illicit drugs the greatest killer of young Vancouverites. Over one death per day in a city with a mere 700,000 residents has traumatized our entire community. That there is no end in sight makes things so much worse.

Statistics are the coldest and least human method by which to understand death, as they obliterate the life story of the individual. Lines on a graph numb your response to the enormous heartbreak caused when one person unexpectedly leaves your life forever. Graphs provide the comfort of the abstract. Stories about real people and personal experiences pull the mind back to reality. For example, one Monday the usual statistical email came into my mayor's inbox, telling me nine people had died the previous week from poisoned drugs and 150 had been revived by firefighters. Statistics told me how this compared with the last week and the week before. It was a little worse than the previous week, but not as bad as it had recently been. This time, though, my mind could not escape the fact that the death of one of my family members was among those recorded in the spreadsheet.

Susan Havelock, my brother-in-law Ray's sister, died from taking toxic drugs early one morning, alone, in the rain, under an awning in Vancouver's Downtown Eastside. Born in 1964, Susan was a loved daughter, sister, mother and friend. She was vivacious, with dreams and hopes for a better future for her and her son. But these were taken from her. Susan died because her drugs were poisoned. She passed away on the street because the drugs she needed were illegal and the substance use disorder with which she lived had made her a criminalized person.

Those who loved Susan struggled to find ways to celebrate her life, as indoor gatherings were prohibited under COVID-19 restrictions. In the end, Ray, his partner (and my sister-in-law), Siobhan Ashe, and I joined about a dozen of Susan's friends outside Vancouver's Drug Treatment Court, where people said kind words through N95 masks. Renowned psychiatrist Dr. Bill MacEwan kindly organized the ceremony and played Creedence Clearwater Revival's version of Dale

Hawkins's song "Susie Q," as it was Ray's nickname for his sister. It didn't seem to be enough, but it was all we were allowed by physical distancing orders as we stood outside in the pouring rain. Ray has given me permission to share the details of Susan's life, because he feels it represents one more thing she did to try and help others despite her own pain. Susan was a very kind, generous and good-hearted person, and she did not deserve this. No one does.

Every person counted and classified by the coroner has a story as tragic as Susan's. Every family who has lost a member to toxic drugs has experienced as much pain. Losses of this kind forever stay with family members and loved ones. Susan's story provides a lesson for all service providers and policy-makers who work in this area but have not lost someone they knew: graphs make sense only when coupled with stories of the dead. When these are combined, they reveal the true horror of what we face here in Vancouver and other communities, and emphasize why change is so necessary.

Sometimes, when I tell people Susan's story, they shrug and say, "I'm so sorry. But you must admit, it was her choice to take drugs. It was her choice to keep using." They rarely have the guts to come right out and say Susan's death was her own fault, feeling content that the implication is sufficient. It is hard to know what to say in the face of such insensitivity, or to understand the person's motivations for such a monstrous response. I learned from living with alcoholics that they drink to feel good, or to stop feeling bad, or to fit in. Most of us know what it is like to have a drink to celebrate or wind down for the day, or because someone offers to buy a round. Fewer people know what it is like to drink to relieve emotional pain and trauma, or what it is like when your body rebels when you sober up, or how hard it is to escape a substance use disorder. There are enough clues to suggest that my father never felt able to fully express his sexuality, which, I have been told, can lead to alcoholism. We will never know. It is hard to know what to do with this knowledge other than to tell the truth as you know it.

Likewise, we may never know why Susan began taking drugs or how she survived for so long in such horrible conditions. But it really shouldn't matter why. What matters is that she was in desperate need of help but was treated like a criminal because of the cruel collective choices we have made as a society. In the minds of the uninformed, Susan should just pull up her socks and obtain treatment, then put behind her whatever demons drive her drug use, and go on to live a long, drug-free, abstinent life. But medical professionals constantly tell us this path is pure fantasy. Susan and so many others living with substance use disorders do access treatment and counselling, but then relapse. If you are a recovering alcoholic who relapses, you go to the bar or liquor store, buy a drink and survive for eighty years like my dad. But illicit drug users are forced back into a world of alleys and organized crime to buy unregulated and now highly toxic drugs to survive. Maybe you will stabilize for a while, maybe you will survive an overdose or two, maybe you will die by yourself at 4 a.m., under an awning in the rain. We collectively killed Susan and so many others by designing our drug policies using bias rather than science.

Canada's First Needle Exchange

Vancouver has a bold history of drug policy reform driven by the pain directly experienced by an extremely brave drug-user community. The story of successful reform usually goes something like this: pressure for change starts when drug users become aware of an emerging threat to their lives, which is then confirmed and reported by the health-care sector, including doctors, nurses, paramedics, peers, non-profit organizations and researchers. Drug users and their health-care allies channel resources to existing services and, if necessary, seek additional funding from local, provincial or federal governments. If the threat continues, the drug-using community will advocate for permissions and policies currently outside the authority of health-care professionals. As will be explained shortly, if refused, drug users often break the law by launching unsanctioned rescue programs. Illegal actions coupled with data-driven reports from health officials increase public awareness and corresponding pressure for formal policy change, which only comes when political actors overcome the incredible inertia of the status quo. People don't like change. Politicians like it even less.

Vancouver is the city that produced the Downtown Eastside Residents Association (DERA) in the 1970s; the Downtown Eastside Youth Activities Society (DEYAS) in the 1980s; the Vancouver Area Network of Drug Users (VANDU) and the Portland Hotel Society (PHS) in the 1990s; and, more recently, the Overdose Prevention Society (OPS), Western Aboriginal Harm Reduction Society (WAHRS) and Drug User Liberation Front (DULF). I am so lucky to include among my friends many people who have worked with these groups, including former city councillor and member of Parliament Libby Davies, who started DERA; Karen Ward from VANDU; Liz Evans, Nathan Allen, Sarah Evans and Jeff West from PHS; Sarah Blyth from OPS; and many more.

Vancouver has so many amazing people who have worked over the years in the health-care sector as doctors, nurses, administrators, front-line workers or researchers. Those who have had a substantive impact on my thinking and actions include chief medical health officer for the City of Vancouver Dr. Patricia Daly, Dr. Kora DeBeck from Simon Fraser University, Vancouver Coastal Health board chair Dr. Penny Ballem, PHS medical director Dr. Christy Sutherland, UBC professor Dr. Mark Tyndall, Vancouver chief constable Adam Palmer, the late Vancouver police department superintendent Bill Spearn, my sister-in-law Mairead Ashe, who is a registered nurse at St. Paul's Hospital in downtown Vancouver, and many others.

Death due to illicit drug use was uncommon in Vancouver prior to the 1980s. There was a small number of recorded cases of heroin-related death, starting in the 1960s, but activists, such as Libby Davies, her partner, Bruce Eriksen, and others from DERA, mainly focused on helping those struggling with alcoholism in their neighbourhood. They fought for access to treatment, but above all they pushed for increasing the quality and supply of affordable housing and services for the Downtown Eastside (DTES) community—mobilizing the community and convincing the City of Vancouver to open the Carnegie Community Centre in the heart of the DTES, on the corner of Main and

Hastings streets, in 1980, to provide needed services for those surviving poverty.

In the late 1980s, three factors converged to dramatically alter the local drug-using environment and turn the DTES into the epicentre of an emerging catastrophe. First, Vancouver hosted the World Exposition on Transportation and Communication in 1986 (Expo 86) and Canada signed the 1988 North American Free Trade Agreement, both of which increased the supply and potency of heroin and cocaine in a city that was until that point far removed from the international drug trade of the day. As a result, many seeking to escape from trauma and pain began using heroin and cocaine instead of, or in addition to, alcohol. This in turn led to increased dependence and criminal activity, because, of course, heroin and cocaine are illegal to possess, deal or traffic, which increases their price and, in turn, pushes drug users to undertake illegal activities to stay well.

Second, many more users began to inject drugs multiple times per day. With heroin, and especially with cocaine, users inject up to ten, twenty or even thirty times per day. This increase in injection frequency requires increased access to needles, which were difficult to find in the 1980s, as dispensing drug paraphernalia was also an illegal activity. The scarcity of needles greatly increased drug users' risk of infection. They were often forced to use unsterilized or shared needles, which became extremely risky because of a third major change to the local drug-using environment: the global HIV/AIDS epidemic.

Drug users and advocates were the first to bring attention to the negative impacts of adapting to the new environment as their friends, neighbours and family members fell ill and died with increasing frequency. One of the first, and strongest, Vancouver voices raising the alarm was local activist John Turvey. A recovering heroin user, Turvey began providing services to youth in need in the early 1980s and formed the Downtown Eastside Youth Activities Society (DEYAS) in 1984. In the late 1980s, Turvey began to break the law by dispensing clean needles and drug paraphernalia in back alleys, using his own money to help prevent the spread of HIV. Health officials, such as the provincially appointed Vancouver chief medical health officer, Dr. John Blatherwick, took heed of Turvey's warnings and began to produce statistics tracking changing public-health patterns as well as advocating for health-care policy reforms, such as free needle exchanges and dispensaries.

Federal and provincial politicians were hostile to these suggested reforms, preferring to continue with a war-on-drugs approach while stigmatizing those contracting HIV. Turvey and Blatherwick approached Vancouver mayor Gordon Campbell of the Non-Partisan Association and the NPA council to help push their initiative forward. Initially reluctant, in 1989 Campbell came to convince Vancouver police chief constable Bob Stewart and the College of Physicians and Surgeons not to oppose the project. Eventually, Campbell also convinced all but two of his fellow NPA councillors to support an initial $100,000 grant to Turvey for DEYAS to run a one-for-one needle exchange program. The two local major daily newspapers wrote coinciding supportive editorials. Mayor Campbell and council did not require provincial permission to provide funding, and did so despite the strong objections of Vancouver voters and centre-right BC Social Credit premier Bill Vander Zalm, who had gone so far as to threaten to fire Blatherwick.

Vancouver's clean-needle programs have proven to be a highly cost-effective method of saving lives by preventing the transmission of HIV and other diseases. Vancouver city council continued funding the needle exchange until a new BC New Democratic Party provincial government, under centre-left premier Michael Harcourt, assumed office in 1991 and expanded similar programs province-wide. Gordon Campbell was re-elected Vancouver mayor in 1990 by a greatly reduced margin of victory and went on to lead the centre-right BC Liberal Party, becoming premier in 2001. Blatherwick received the Order of Canada in 1994 for his work in assisting people living with AIDS. Turvey was appointed to the Order of Canada for his advocacy in 2006.

Insite

The origin story of North America's first supervised consumption site—Insite—has been told many times, including in an extremely watchable 2002 film, *Fix: The Story of an Addicted City*, directed by Nettie Wild, and in Travis Lupick's excellent 2017 book, *Fighting for Space*. What is worth repeating is how the opening of Insite followed a path like that taken to secure Turvey's needle exchange. First, external shocks changed the fundamental nature of the drug-using environment and people began to fall ill and die. Local activists then began to call for immediate assistance and policy reform, and local public health officials quickly did what they could within their authority, including joining the call for new federal and provincial programs and policies. Municipalities came to join the calls for senior government action, but change did not come until sympathetic federal and provincial politicians emerged to lead the efforts to overcome the status quo.

As we've seen, drug users began to die at a higher-than-normal rate in Vancouver in the late 1980s. While the efforts of John Turvey and others to bring clean needles to Vancouver's Downtown Eastside had significantly reduced HIV transmissions, this measure did little to impact deaths specifically due to illicit drug use. The rising death toll was obvious to the local community, who began taking matters into their own hands by voluntarily, and without permission, undertaking measures that are now commonly referred to as "harm reduction." Early harm-reduction measures involved proponents of this approach, such as Liz Evans and Mark Townsend, who began managing and working at Vancouver's run-down Pennsylvania Hotel in 1991, allowing drugs to be sold, purchased and consumed in their facilities, distributing drug paraphernalia, administering first aid, and asking people to leave their room doors open while using so staff and neighbours could take life-saving action in the event of overdose. In other words, Evans and Townsend were basically operating an unauthorized supervised consumption site on their premises.

The unauthorized and often illegal actions of Evans, Townsend and many others proved to be helpful, but ultimately not enough, to counter the wave of death in the DTES and, increasingly, in other BC communities. Overdose death rates continued to rise and come to the attention of public health officials, with almost four people per week dying of illicit drug-related deaths in 1993, when the death rate exceeded forty people per 100,000—three times the rate of the previous year. In 1993, British Columbia chief coroner Vince Cain requested that the BC attorney general authorize a task force under Cain's direction to review and make recommendations regarding "the nature, causes, and extent of untimely and unnatural deaths resulting from the use and abuse of narcotic drugs."[14]

Published in 1994, what came to be known as the Cain Report documented the extent and probable causes of these overdose deaths. Cain's report is built on the idea of a "harm reduction model," which had been growing in acceptance since the 1980s in Canada and elsewhere. The central premise of harm reduction is to "reduce the negative consequences associated with drug use rather than the traditional focus of reducing the prevalence of drug use." Radically, his report recommended expanding harm reduction services, such as drug-paraphernalia provision and treatment centres, as well as "decriminalizing the possession and use of specified substances by people shown to be addicted to those specific substances," and seriously inquiring "into the merits of legalizing the possession of some of the so-called 'soft-drugs,' such as marijuana."

Drug users and advocates increased unauthorized harm-reduction measures as the death toll continued to rise. They also began to organize and harness the power of collective action to promote policy change. In 1995, a local activist named Ann Livingston started organizing drug users, and in April of that year the group IV Feed began to meet in a dilapidated building in Vancouver they called the Back Alley.[15] Operating with small amounts of funding from various local individuals and non-governmental organizations, street nurses made regular calls to the facility, and the police largely left the Back Alley alone as long as things kept quiet. It was shut in 1996 when funding dried up after drug dealers operating on the premises prompted a police raid. Livingston continued to organize drug users, working with DTES poet Bud Osborn to form an important new non-profit organization called the Vancouver Area Network of Drug Users (VANDU). In 1998, VANDU developed a plan for the local health authority to set up four "safe injection sites" in Vancouver's Downtown Eastside. This plan was rejected by the Vancouver/ Richmond Health Authority (now Vancouver Coastal Health, or VCH). This roadblock did not stop VANDU, which then set up its own unsanctioned sites in portable washrooms. The Vancouver police would shut down the VANDU sites, which VANDU would reopen once the coast was clear.

This unauthorized and radical activity began to catch the attention of municipal officials, some of whom became very unlikely allies. Centre-right NPA mayor of Vancouver Philip Owen and his council candidates swept to power in 1993, winning the mayoralty and nine of ten council seats. Owen was very much a law-and-order mayor through his first three-year term, dramatically increasing police funding despite other budgetary pressures. But he began to develop a deeper understanding of the issue in his second term, starting in 1996 with Owen's NPA winning every Vancouver council, park board and school board seat. Owen hired DTES Carnegie

Community Centre coordinator Donald MacPherson in 1997 as the city's first drug policy coordinator, tasked with exploring a new approach to drug policy that eventually led to the City of Vancouver adopting its renowned "four-pillar" approach to harm reduction. Despite his increasing interest in drug policy reform, voters still supported Owen, who was re-elected in 1999, when his NPA party secured eight of ten council positions.

Champions for harm reduction also began to emerge at the federal and provincial levels of government. In March 2000, Mayor Owen, federal secretary of state for western economic diversification Ronald Duhamel, federal secretary of state for multiculturalism and the status of women Dr. Hedy Fry, and BC minister of community development, cooperatives and volunteers Jenny Kwan all signed the Vancouver Agreement on behalf of their governments. Focusing on the DTES, the Vancouver Agreement named common areas of interest where Canada's three levels of government agreed to co-operate to provide organizational and financial support for local community solutions to economic, social, health and safety issues.

These developments culminated in Donald MacPherson's suggested reforms contained in *A Framework for Action: A Four-Pillar Approach to Drug Problems in Vancouver*. Based on two years of research and community consultation, the report was presented to Vancouver city council in May 2001 for their consideration and endorsement. The report recommended supporting harm reduction measures such as setting up a multi-sectoral task force "to consider the feasibility of a scientific medical project to develop safe injection sites or supervised consumption facilities in Vancouver...to reduce health risks and minimize open drug scenes."[16] The report was unanimously approved by Owen's right-of-centre council colleagues—grudgingly by some.

Despite voting for his four-pillar plan, Owen's NPA colleagues were unhappy and worked to oust him as mayor. As is recounted in the 2009 book *A Thousand Dreams: Vancouver's Downtown Eastside and the Fight for Its Future*, by Larry Campbell, Neil Boyd and Lori Culbert, the NPA party brass broke with tradition and informed Owen he would have to stand against other candidates for nomination if he wanted to serve as mayor for a fourth term, in response to an outcry from Chinatown merchants and others opposed to Owen's four-pillar strategy. Taken by surprise, Owen stood down as a candidate after discovering that NPA councillor (and eventual 2002 NPA mayoral candidate) Jennifer Clarke had been organizing for months to oust him as the NPA's mayoral candidate.

Owen's ouster opened the door for centre-left COPE mayoral candidate Larry Campbell, former RCMP officer, chief coroner of British Columbia and the inspiration for the hit TV series *Da Vinci's Inquest*. With the NPA hopelessly divided after Owen's betrayal, a brilliant campaign by manager Neil Monckton saw Larry Campbell elected Vancouver mayor in November 2002. Campbell promised during the campaign to open a new supervised consumption site within months of being elected. Now centre-left Mayor Campbell worked to bring centre-right BC Liberal premier Gordon Campbell onside, thus giving Vancouver Coastal Health the support it needed to apply for an exemption to

Section 56 of Canada's Controlled Drugs and Substances Act in early 2003. Canada's federal health minister granted the exemption in September 2003, and Insite opened as the first officially sanctioned site for the consumption of illicit drugs in North America. Since it opened, there have been more than 3.6 million nurse-supervised visits to inject illicit drugs, 6,440 overdose interventions, and not a single death. Other authorized supervised-consumption sites were later opened, and illicit drug–related deaths in Vancouver stabilized for the next decade, thanks to Insite and other harm reduction measures.

As mentioned above, illicit drug–related deaths in Vancouver were rare prior to the 1990s, but began to rapidly increase because of external shocks to drug users' local environment. The needle exchange and Insite opened only after local activists teamed up with local health-care professionals to take what actions they could to save lives and call for more government action. Governments initially opposed these policy suggestions, but then municipal government actors dropped their opposition and began to push for change, eventually to be followed by federal and provincial governments.

Vancouver city council could, on its own, enable the needle exchange program, as it required no aid or approval from the federal or provincial governments, but merely municipal funding and an agreement from police not to interfere with the program's operation. Insite was far more complicated. It required formal approval by the Vancouver health authority and the federal government, as well as informal municipal and provincial support. While both of these facilities were hard-won and very important, the federal and provincial governments continued to maintain their overall war-on-drugs policy framework, which would become even more entrenched in the coming years.

4

FROM DESOLATION TO HOPE TO DISAPPOINTMENT

I WAS ELECTED TO CANADA'S NATIONAL PARLIAMENT IN 2011 AS the centre-left New Democratic Party member for Burnaby–Douglas. Progressive drug policy reform of any type was not on the political agenda when I took my seat in the House of Commons. Conservative prime minister Stephen Harper's newly elected centre-right majority government was ramping up Canada's war on drug users. Also undertaking "a war on science," Harper went all out to muzzle scientists and researchers, shut down supervised consumption sites like Insite, and enact mandatory minimum sentences for drug possession. It was a very dark four years for those believing government policy should be based on the best possible research and drug policy reform advocacy.

In the 2015 election, Liberal leader Justin Trudeau proposed a radical departure from Harper's century-old approach to criminalizing drug users by declaring he would legalize cannabis if elected prime minister. Trudeau used this and other left-leaning policy promises to secure a majority government in the House of Commons for the traditionally centrist Liberal Party. I was re-elected as member of Parliament in 2015 and took part in the parliamentary process through which cannabis was legalized. While this was a massive drug policy change, the debate about cannabis left no political space for other conversations regarding controlled and illicit drug policy reform, even as illicit drug-related deaths skyrocketed in Vancouver and across British Columbia.

Hope for further drug policy reform returned to Ottawa in 2017, when Canada's new NDP leader Jagmeet Singh radically broke with the party's past policy by declaring he supported decriminalizing the personal possession of small quantities of controlled and illicit drugs. Singh's idea picked up steam when Liberal Party convention delegates voted to make decriminalization official party policy a few months later. However, the idea appeared deader than a doornail when, in 2018, Prime Minister Trudeau declared he was opposed to decriminalization, just as I resigned my seat in the House of Commons and entered the race to become the next mayor of Vancouver. Ironically, the path forward for decriminalizing hard drugs appeared initially blocked by the same man who legalized cannabis.

Harper's War on Drugs

In 2011, I was elected to Parliament with Jack Layton's NDP when our 103 MPs rode an orange wave (the NDP's official colour) to become official opposition to Stephen Harper's new Conservative majority government. Under Layton's leadership, the NDP secured the most seats in its history, owing to his appeal to regular Canadians and his willingness to fight for issues about which they cared. I remember the euphoria I felt on the evening of May 2, 2011, when the media reported I had been elected by a mere 1,011 votes over my Conservative opponent. It had been a tough campaign. It started with a contested party nomination where I, helped by my wife, Jeanette Ashe, my brother, Evan Stewart, and a small team, became the official local NDP candidate. I will never forget when the NDP held a rally in my home constituency of Burnaby–Douglas on Saturday, April 30, three days before general election day, where Jack Layton, who had been recovering from cancer treatments, held his cane aloft and helped me and so many other NDP candidates get across the finish line.

I also remember the crushing feeling we had, huddled in our ramshackle campaign office on Hastings Street in Burnaby, after hearing that Prime Minister Stephen Harper had secured a Conservative majority. Sure, we had a democratic-socialist official opposition for the first time in history under Jack Layton, whose values matched my own, but also a terrifying new neo-conservative majority government bent on radical change. After being granted a generous leave of absence from Simon Fraser University's School of Public Policy, where I served as a tenured associate professor of political science, I was soon off to Ottawa for a political adventure in the institution I had studied for so many years.

I remember Layton calling me a few days after the election to ask which critic area would interest me. I said finance without a moment's hesitation—brazenly thinking I would be an excellent official opposition finance critic to Harper's venerable finance minister, Jim Flaherty, despite having no experience. In the end, I was appointed official opposition critic for the Western Economic Diversification Agency and assigned a seat on the Standing Committee on Justice and Human Rights, in what I now see as quite generous appointments.

I look back at my big ego and naïveté with embarrassment, especially since the NDP would soon enter a period of extreme pain and crisis. I remember sitting in the seat behind Layton when he delivered what would be his last speech in the House of Commons, as the cancer he had fought for so long had now returned. Jack spoke with passion for an hour against the Harper government's decision to lock Canada Post workers out of their workplaces. He eloquently outlined the core of our argument to show his huge crew of rookie NDP MPs how to properly act in the House of Commons. He did this with sweat pouring down his back, leaning on his desk for support. Inspiring. He had dedicated his life to making Canada a better place for regular people, and we are all the poorer for his untimely death. His passing was sudden and jarring. The parliamentary session began on June 2, Jack temporarily stepped down as leader on July 25, and he died on August 22, 2011. Then the party fell into chaos.

The Liberal Party was also in disarray after losing so badly in the 2015 election. Liberal MPs were very grumpy with their third-party status, and they were in the midst of yet another leadership race. But Prime Minister Harper had a majority, and the Conservatives got right to work with his

agenda, pushing a huge number of bills through Parliament—
including his 2012 omnibus budget entitled the Jobs, Growth
and Long-Term Prosperity Act that gutted Canada's environmental laws and stripped millions of dollars from essential
programs. The Conservatives also brought in the Safe Streets
and Communities Act, which entrenched Ronald Reagan-
esque, neo-conservative drug policies, including mandatory
minimum sentences for possessing six or more marijuana
plants.[17] Harper also ramped up his war on drug users
by attempting to shut down Vancouver's Insite and prevent new supervised consumption sites from opening.[18] It
was a bleak four years for social justice under the Harper
Conservative majority.

Nycole Turmel held the interim NDP leadership position
between July 2011 and March 2012, until NDP MP Thomas
Mulcair was selected by party members as the party's new
permanent leader. A lawyer, Mulcair was a sight to behold
in the House of Commons, especially during question period, where he excelled in holding Prime Minister Harper
to account by asking penetrating, prosecutorial-style questions. I could clearly see Harper would rather be anywhere
else than in the House of Commons answering Mulcair's
questions about scandals involving his chief of staff, Nigel
Wright, or disgraced senators whom Harper had appointed.
It was something else to watch from my ringside, but middle-
bencher, seat. Mulcair held more socially conservative views
than Layton. For example, as far back as 2004, Layton joked
"some might say I never exhaled" when asked if he smoked
cannabis, whereas Mulcair, when asked the same question
a decade later, acknowledged past cannabis use but then

descended into legalistic answers portraying a much less progressive stance. To be fair, Mulcair deeply opposed Harper's mandatory minimum sentences for cannabis possession.

I was with a small number of MPs who had backed second-place finisher Brian Topp during the NDP leadership race, so I was already not in Mulcair's good books. Things quickly went from bad to worse for me within the NDP organization, as I had also begun what often seemed like a one–MP, six-year crusade to stop the federal government from permitting the Texas-based oil pipeline company Kinder Morgan to twin its existing Trans Mountain crude-oil pipeline (TMX). The proposed pipeline would transport 300,000 barrels of crude oil per day from the Alberta tar sands to oil tankers off the west coast of British Columbia. I did not have permission from Turmel, or later Mulcair, to oppose this pipeline and was told many times to stop, but I continued to reflect the opinions of my constituents and the First Nations through whose unceded territories TMX was projected to pass.

While the federal NDP officially opposed the Enbridge Northern Gateway Pipeline slated to run through Northern British Columbia, and the proposal to build the Keystone XL Pipeline from Alberta to the United States, it was not officially opposed to TMX. I was told the federal NDP remained neutral on TMX, as it was supported by Alberta provincial NDP leader, and eventually premier, Rachel Notley, as well as by BC NDP leader Adrian Dix and his energy critic, and later BC NDP premier, John Horgan, although Dix came to publicly express his opposition to the project in 2013. I was banned from asking questions in the House of Commons about TMX and from speaking to the media on the topic, but I continued to voice my opposition using privileges guaranteed to all MPs, such as petitioning. I also worked with NGOs like Stand.earth and Dogwood to organize protests in my Burnaby riding, and with First Nations up and down the proposed pipeline route—particularly the Tsleil-Waututh First Nation, in whose territories my constituency was located and for whom my brother, Evan, worked, with Chief Leah George-Wilson.

While Mulcair continued holding Prime Minister Harper to account, and Harper's Conservative majority government continued to pass regressive laws, the Liberal Party was starting to get its act together. In April 2013, Justin Trudeau cruised to victory to become the new Liberal Party leader, replacing Michael Ignatieff, who had failed to connect with voters and crashed and burned during the 2011 election. Many initially viewed Trudeau as a political lightweight—especially Mulcair, who often mocked him at the NDP's Wednesday morning caucus meetings, calling Trudeau "the Dauphin." The NDP leadership team firmly bought into the "Stop Harper" campaign and never formulated a strategy just in case Trudeau's popularity began to increase. Leaving our left flank open for the Liberals to exploit would prove a critical error in the next election.

In early August 2015, Mulcair looked poised to become Canada's next prime minister. He led in the polls by as much as ten percentage points over Harper's Conservatives and by fifteen percentage points over Trudeau's third-place Liberals. This all changed as Trudeau leapfrogged over Mulcair to land on his left on several key policy areas—including drug policy. During the 2015 election, seemingly to everyone's surprise,

Trudeau promised to legalize cannabis.[19] Caught off-guard, Mulcair repeated his pledge to decriminalize, but not legalize, cannabis.[20] This brilliant move by Justin Trudeau to woo NDP voters came at no real political cost, as by this time most Canadians thought it was too harsh to throw people in jail for smoking or selling pot. He had taken a page out of the playbook of his father, former Liberal prime minister Pierre Elliott Trudeau, by championing a big social-justice issue that was inexpensive to implement but brought those who suffered under unjust laws into the Liberal camp. Pierre Trudeau did it by removing the state from the "bedrooms of the nation," reforming laws concerning abortion, divorce and homosexuality. Justin Trudeau used cannabis legalization to the same effect.

What perhaps seemed like a surprise move to average voters during the 2015 election had really been a long time in the making. Liberal Party members had voted to support cannabis legalization at the January 2012 Liberal convention.[21] Later that year, during the Liberal leadership race, Justin Trudeau said he had changed his mind on cannabis legalization and was now in favour. In November 2012, Trudeau said, "I've certainly evolved from conversations with supporters and Liberals. I am fully a supporter of decriminalization. I think the time has come for that. I am actually very open to legalization and specifically tax and regulation the way they are calling it in the States. It's something I am looking forward to having a lot of serious discussion about."[22] This willingness to listen and be open to risking policy change is one of Trudeau's great strengths and one of the keys to his success.

Cannabis and other gambles paid off for Trudeau, especially his openness to running deficits to provide enhanced public services, compared with Mulcair's out-of-touch promise to deliver consecutive balanced budgets.[23] On October 19, 2015, the Liberals cruised to a 184-seat majority. Harper dropped from 166 to 99 seats, and the Mulcair-led NDP fell from 103 to 44 seats. I had mixed feelings on election night, just like in 2011. It had been a gruelling eleven-week campaign, and a boundary adjustment meant that I had to stand for re-election in a newly constituted constituency. I had a good team, with Jeanette and Evan at my side as always, and veteran NDP organizer Krystal Smith as my campaign manager. But by 2015, Jack Layton's orange wave had given way to Trudeau's red tide. Only our months of record-level fundraising and door-knocking saved my seat from the Liberals.[24] Even so, Burnaby South was the last seat declared in the country, and the media had initially reported my Liberal opponent, Adam Pankratz, as the winner. In what must have been a devastating shock ending, Pankratz's win was reversed in the media when the advance votes were eventually counted, and I was re-elected by a mere 547 votes.

I was sent back to the House of Commons by a whisker, but, crushingly, well over half of my NDP MP colleagues lost their seats. Canadians had managed to "stop Harper" and vote in a progressive government, but at a cost of the NDP dropping down to become only the third-largest party in the House of Commons. I was relieved that Trudeau, rather than Harper, was now at the helm, but it did not mean I would stop fighting for social and environmental justice from the opposition benches.

Trudeau Lights Up Cannabis

It was exciting, but bittersweet, to be back in the House of Commons in December 2015 as the curtain lifted on the Trudeau era. Stephen Harper sitting on the opposition benches was a welcome sight, as were all the Liberal MPs on the government side—many of whom had very progressive attitudes. I had developed good working relationships with many of those I had served with in the previous Parliament, and I now had opportunities to influence government policy despite being assigned minor roles by Mulcair in our greatly diminished party.

What quickly became apparent was that the Liberals were very pleased to be back in government after almost a decade out of power. Very, very pleased. Prime Minister Trudeau spent many months parading around the country and world proclaiming, "Canada is back" and "I am a feminist" while doing little to substantiate these claims. The Liberals squandered almost two years of their majority mandate talking up all the things they were going to do and not doing much to get them done. It appeared Trudeau's Liberals were more about rhetoric than real, substantive change. Four years is not much time to implement an agenda, and new governments must make each day count. Harper certainly did when he and his majority hit the ground running in 2011, but Trudeau, to use a common saying from where I grew up, in Nova Scotia's Annapolis Valley, "moved slower than cold molasses going up a hill in January." There was certainly not much happening on the drug file in the early years of the Trudeau mandate, despite all the 2015 election talk.

NDP members were understandably very upset with Mulcair after the 2015 election catastrophe. He started the campaign with the realistic expectation of forming government but finished with the all-too-familiar third-party status. Members were especially distraught because the centrist Liberals did it by promising progressive policies considered by many to be traditional NDP terrain. Unfortunately for Mulcair, an NDP constitutional clause stipulating biennial conventions triggered an April 2016 national meeting that would come to include a vote on his leadership. Like others, I was firmly for change. I had not backed Mulcair during the 2012 NDP leadership race, frequently clashed with him in caucus meetings, and was awarded only minor portfolios under his leadership. I admired him in the House of Commons, but thought he paid little attention to party management or public outreach. As a result, I worked with others to unseat him at the April convention and was hopeful for positive change. Despite the passing of the vote to change leaders, I was alarmed and disappointed when Mulcair stayed on as leader for nearly two more years as members chose his successor.

A successful political leader must excel in three key areas: campaigning, management and public speaking. In terms of campaigning, a leader must understand the mechanics of what it takes to win and be able to entice hundreds of thousands of people to vote, volunteer, join the party and donate. As for management, leaders need to understand how to implement their mission and build caucus and internal staff teams that can get the work done. Finally, a successful leader must also deliver strong performances week in and week out for their caucus, opposition, media and the public.

Every leader will have strengths and weaknesses, but, in my view, they must master at least two of these three categories, and be adequate in the third, to succeed.

In 2011, NDP leader Jack Layton was great in all three required areas and was rewarded with a massive seat increase. He had been continuously running in elections for thirty years and knew how to win. He had built a seasoned and talented team to propel his leadership ambitions. He was convincing to hundreds of thousands of Canadians who believed he was on their side, and could animate crowds like few others. Conservative Stephen Harper also deeply understood campaigns, using a very targeted approach to secure just enough public support to win his majority. He was a true management genius and avoided as much public speaking as he could, while performing decently when pressed. Liberal leader Michael Ignatieff's aristocratic persona ticked none of the three boxes and he was brutally punished at the polls for it.

Harper's targeted campaign approach failed him in 2015, and although he still managed his team very well, he was no match for Mulcair or, to everyone's surprise, Trudeau when it came to public speaking. Trudeau hired the very talented Katie Telford and Gerald Butts to take care of his campaigning and management duties, in which, in my opinion, he had little direct interest in those early years. Trudeau placed most of his attention on public performance, which the public came to prefer to Harper's and Mulcair's. Mulcair never embraced campaigning, cared little about management, but excelled as a parliamentarian. Delivering only one of three key leadership aspects and sliding so far back in terms of seats won led to over half of the seventeen hundred delegated NDP party members at the wild April 2016 party convention to reject him as leader.[25]

I was excited when Ontario member of provincial parliament and criminal defence lawyer Jagmeet Singh decided to put his name forward for federal NDP leader during the 2017 leadership selection contest. Although NDP MP and good friend Randall Garrison got there first, I was the second MP to support Singh's leadership bid. I thought he would attract more supporters than the other candidates, especially younger people and those from minority groups. I quickly discovered that party management and administration were not his strong points, although I thought him a good enough speaker to hold his own in the House of Commons (but not nearly as strong as his leadership rival, Charlie Angus). I spent considerable time working on his campaign and then putting together a detailed transition plan to help him succeed as soon as he won the contest on October 1, 2017.

Singh was the first federal party leader to openly advocate decriminalizing all drugs, and the first true champion of this policy change on the federal scene. During the 2017 leadership race, Singh said that if elected leader, "I would call for the immediate decriminalization of all personal possession offences when it comes to drugs. Period. It's not acceptable in our country. It's something that doesn't actually help our country and what it does is it criminalizes those that are already worse off in society."[26]

The Trudeau government was finally moving forward with legalizing cannabis at the same time as the NDP was picking its new leader. In April 2017, federal minister of

justice and attorney general Jody Wilson-Raybould introduced Bill C-45, the Cannabis Act, in the House of Commons.
The government bill proposed allowing the legal production,
distribution and sale of cannabis to deter criminal activity and reduce the burden on the criminal justice system.
Responding to reporters' questions concerning the Cannabis
Act in September 2017, Trudeau said he was "not looking at
decriminalization or legalization of any other drugs other
than what we are doing with marijuana...We are going to
focus on getting the control and regulation of [the] marijuana
regime right. And that is quite a handful right now and we are
not looking at any other steps."[27] And that would appear to be
that: case closed on other possible drug policy reforms.

The Cannabis Act easily passed through the House of
Commons and was sent to the Senate for consideration in
November 2017. The bill had a rough ride in the Conservative-
controlled Senate, requiring back-and-forth negotiations
with the Trudeau government before it was approved by a
majority of senators. On June 21, 2018, Speaker Geoff Regan
entered the House of Commons and walked to his imposing
chair to start the proceedings of the day. He informed the
sparsely filled chamber that the Cannabis Act would receive
royal assent after passing third reading in the Senate. Later
that day, cannabis again became a legal substance for the
first time in almost one hundred years.

Activists complained that the Cannabis Act did not go far
enough and that it focused too much on continuing to punish drug-related activities. However, it represents the most
significant reversal of federal drug policy since the federal
government under the leadership of Liberal prime minister

Wilfrid Laurier brought in the 1908 Opium Act, which criminalized first hard drugs and then cannabis, after it was added to the list of prohibited substances in 1923 by Liberal prime minister William Lyon Mackenzie King.[28] The Cannabis Act flies in the face of decades of successive Conservative and Liberal governments either ignoring the harms brought by prohibition or, worse, further entrenching war-on-drug policies. Re-legalizing cannabis is a massive step forward for Canadians. If in doubt, ask one of the 250,000 Canadians with existing drug possession convictions stemming from cannabis possession. Ask them about how it has needlessly and negatively impacted their travel, employment or police interactions. Really listen carefully to the Indigenous, racialized and poor people who have been disproportionately affected by discriminatory laws.

While I was glad cannabis was now legal, I was going through significant soul-searching about what I was doing with my life. Despite my support for Jagmeet Singh during the leadership campaign, I was reappointed as official opposition science critic for the NDP and not promoted to a more challenging role, which I craved. Jeanette and I loved the Ottawa buzz, but I felt I had reached my ceiling within the party and was ready to return to academia. Then a new, unexpected political opportunity appeared in Vancouver.

5

"WE ARE NOT GOING TO DECRIMINALIZE DRUGS"

I MADE MY LAST SPEECH IN PARLIAMENT JUST DAYS BEFORE Prime Minister Trudeau re-legalized cannabis in June 2018. I announced I was stepping down as MP for Burnaby South as I watched the sunlight stream through the magnificent stained-glass windows in the House of Commons for the last time, after spending seven years in my seat. Little did I know that much of the next four years of my life would involve working with other drug policy reformers to save lives, not as an MP, but as the fortieth mayor of Vancouver. For years, Trudeau and the Liberal cabinet worked hard to stamp out any discussion of decriminalization, and even while activists, health officials and politicians outside his inner circle of ministers were making it harder to do so, Trudeau continued saying no—including twice to my face.

Off the Table

The Cannabis Act marked a significant step down the drug liberalization path but also stifled further drug policy reform debate. After all, Trudeau had delivered on his 2015 election promise and pushed through the most significant drug policy reform in the country's history. It appeared he thought he had done enough on the drug policy liberalization file. This is a totally understandable position. The prime minister does not operate in a political vacuum. In politics, it is not simply about doing the right thing, but rather doing the right thing in the context of what your opponent proposes they will do—and drug policy reform is a very tricky issue to play around with. Go too far toward the health-centred approach and you risk losing nervous centrist voters. Go too far down the war-on-drugs path and you risk losing compassionate centrist voters. Science matters, but in politics, votes matter more.

Trudeau's cannabis risk paid off in 2015, as his stance helped pull enough votes away from Mulcair's NDP to oust Stephen Harper's Conservative Party. Trudeau's newest opponent, Andrew Scheer, who served as Conservative Party leader from May 2017 to August 2020, slightly modified the Conservatives' approach toward cannabis. Instead of saying the Conservatives would roll back legalization, Scheer officially opposed the Cannabis Act as being rushed, not ready and too permissive, later saying he would not reverse the policy if he became prime minister.[29] Instead, Scheer opened a new attack, claiming the Liberals planned to legalize heroin, thus making it dangerous for Trudeau to explore policy reform beyond cannabis.[30]

While the debate on more extensive drug policy reform was stalled around the Trudeau cabinet table, decriminalization was at least part of the conversation among activists and politicians outside the prime minister's inner circle. The full horror of the 2016 toxic drug–related public health emergency was making some of British Columbia premier John Horgan's minority cabinet nervous as they scrambled to develop credible talking points to shield them from criticism. BC NDP minister of mental health and addictions Judy Darcy even hinted the province might be interested in supporting federal policy change when, in September 2017, she advocated for a "national conversation" about decriminalizing heroin, cocaine and other drugs. Many federal Liberal Party members felt emboldened by their cannabis legalization triumph and began to pursue more aggressive drug policy changes, in part reacting to federal NDP leader Jagmeet Singh's pro–drug decriminalization stance, which repositioned the party ahead of the Liberals on the drug issue in the eyes of progressive voters. But there was not yet a formal route allowing these pressures to vent, as the prime minister and his cabinet kept blocking any attempt to move forward.

Additional pressure to move on this issue fell on Trudeau. In February 2018, the federal NDP officially adopted its new leader Singh's campaign promise and passed a party conference resolution to end the criminalization of the personal possession of all drugs.[31] Partially unnerved by the NDP's bold move, a delegation led by MP Nathaniel Erskine-Smith at the April 2018 federal Liberal Party convention managed to convince party members to pass a resolution declaring "the

Government of Canada should treat drug abuse as a health issue, expand treatment and harm reduction services and re-classify low-level drug possession and consumption as administrative violations."[32]

Trudeau and his cabinet stood firm, despite these new developments. When asked about Erskine-Smith's convention motion, Minister of Justice and Attorney General Jody Wilson-Raybould stated, "We are focused on cannabis. We are not moving forward with any other decriminalization."[33] Prime Minister Trudeau and Health Minister Ginette Petitpas Taylor reinforced this message in later media interviews. As the window for decriminalization slammed shut in Ottawa, another was opening in Vancouver.

(Very) Unlikely Mayor

During the 2017 Christmas holidays I had many chats with Jeanette and decided I would not stand for re-election for the NDP in the upcoming 2019 federal election. By this point I had done the best I could with the position I had, winning two close elections, serving Burnaby constituents, mentoring dedicated staff, bringing electronic petitioning to the House of Commons, fighting the good fight against the TMX pipeline expansion, and making lifelong friends. I personally needed to do something different and had decided to return to Simon Fraser University's School of Public Policy, from which I was on leave. Just when I had settled on returning to the ivory tower of academia, three-term Vision Vancouver mayor Gregor Robertson announced he would not stand in the November 2018 civic election, and a new opportunity presented itself.

I became increasingly curious about standing for mayor, even though I knew there were plenty of potential candidates far ahead of me in the cue. I cared a lot about Vancouver, as I had lived there or in Burnaby since moving to the West Coast from Nova Scotia in the 1980s. I had worked as a planning assistant at the City of Vancouver, written numerous academic articles about city politics, and worked in local elections. However, as a Burnaby-based MP, I had no real or recent connections with local Vancouver parties, and I knew Vision Vancouver was not keen on me because I had publicly criticized Vision mayor Robertson for failing to keep his clear and repeated promise to end homelessness by 2015. I now look back at my criticism and cringe. Upon reflection, I can now see centre-left mayors Gregor Robertson and Mike Harcourt as Vancouver's best civic leaders, who accomplished groundbreaking things for the city under tough circumstances.

While the possibility of running for mayor was floating around, the fight against the TMX pipeline expansion reached a new height as thousands of protesters marched to Burnaby in March 2018 to stop the expansion of an oil tank farm needed to facilitate exporting 300,000 barrels of tar-sands crude oil per day by tanker through Burrard Inlet to open waters. TMX proponent and tank farm owner Kinder Morgan obtained a court injunction protecting their worksite on Burnaby Mountain, and violators began to be arrested and charged. I had been deeply involved with the community in organizing against the pipeline for years, and at one meeting Stewart Phillip, the legendary president of the Union of British Columbia Indian Chiefs, took me aside, saying, "Speeches are fine, but now it is time to put your money where your mouth is." A strong challenge from one of the greatest modern Indigenous leaders.

On March 23, 2018, federal Green Party leader Elizabeth May and I stood at the gates of Kinder Morgan's Burnaby oil tank farm and held hands with several other protesters, blocking trucks and construction workers as they approached to start their work for the day. The Burnaby Royal Canadian Mounted Police read us the court injunction and told us we would be arrested if we did not allow the convoy to pass. We said we would not move, and the police told us they were now going to arrest us. Elizabeth May started singing "O Canada" and several police officers wept as they arrested their own member of Parliament. I had no idea how the arrest would affect my life. A team of lawyers headed by the highly regarded Richard Fowler prepared our defence. On May 14, I pleaded guilty to criminal contempt of court and was fined $500. Upon leaving the court I sincerely felt I had respected the wishes of Indigenous people and settlers opposed to the pipeline to the best of my ability and had done all I could to stop what I thought from the get-go was a terrible project.

At the same time as my arrest and court appearances, I began calling others whom I had heard were considering putting their names forward to stand as Vancouver mayor, to see if I could help their bids. I thought my arrest and conviction seriously limited my chances of becoming mayor, but wanted to help Vancouver city hall remain in good hands after Robertson finished his term. I started with retired NDP

MP and mentor Libby Davies, who had stood for mayor in 1993. When Davies decided not to run, I approached sitting Vancouver NDP MP Don Davies (no relation), who, after much hand-wringing, declared he would stay on in Ottawa. In April, Shauna Sylvester, a former Vision Vancouver board member and director of Simon Fraser University's Morris J. Wosk Centre for Dialogue, became the first official candidate for mayor, declaring she would stand as an independent candidate and not for Vision Vancouver. Her decision to run as an independent, centrist candidate played a significant role in my later victory.

A May 3, 2018, poll suggested I was in the running to become mayor, but far behind potential candidates like Vancouver Green Party leader and two-term city councillor Adriane Carr.[34] We had several discussions, but her stalling strongly suggested she was not serious about putting her name forward, and that a path was opening for me to run. Despite the long odds, I brought together a small team of Jeanette, Neil Monckton, SFU public policy professor Doug McArthur and union organizer Nathan Allen to explore my possible candidacy. On May 10, 2018, I kicked off my campaign for mayor by promising to tackle the affordable housing crisis and keep the right wing out of city hall.

The race became more crowded as private health-care business owner Ken Sim was selected to stand as the centre-right Non-Partisan Association mayoral candidate, and hereditary chief of the Squamish First Nation Ian Campbell entered the race as the centrist Vision Vancouver's replacement for Gregor Robertson. Other new parties and mayoral candidates continued to join the mayoral contest over the next few weeks. Much to my delight, a June 14 poll showed me with a slight lead in a tightly packed field of aspiring mayors.[35] I was also heartened when the Vancouver and District Labour Council voted to support my candidacy. That the main labour organization in the city, including unions representing over fifty thousand workers, had my back really helped me gain credibility, but my victory was still very far from assured.

Much to everyone's surprise, Ian Campbell dropped out of the race on September 10 because of past and undisclosed personal difficulties. With just over a month before voting day, the polls showed I was starting to pull away from the pack, with the NPA's Ken Sim as my closest competitor. On September 18, 2018, I formally resigned as the MP for Burnaby South and filed my paperwork to become an official mayoral candidate.[36]

I made dramatically increasing affordable housing the centrepiece of my campaign, as concerns about housing dominated public domain polling, and my rival Ken Sim's main plan for housing was merely to increase the number of basement suites so homeowners could benefit from what Sim called "mortgage helpers"—otherwise known as low-income renters. By late September, I knew I had to address drug-related deaths but did not have a clear idea of what to do. I was nervous about discussing drug policy, as I felt my pipeline arrest and being a member of Parliament for the democratic socialist NDP would alienate the moderate-centrist voters I felt I needed to win. As such, on September 20, I took the politically palatable way out, and instead of committing to specific reforms, I promised to immediately strike a task force if elected, to consider "initiating a safe and accessible supply of drugs for those at high risk in the current illegal and dangerous market, expanding safe consumption sites, and new fentanyl alert testing facilities."[37] Former NDP MP Libby Davies once again had my back and hosted the corresponding media event, and I was very grateful to well-known drug-user advocates Karen Ward and Dean Wilson for attending.[38]

The issue of decriminalizing drugs arose only once during the campaign, when intrepid *Globe and Mail* reporter Andrea Woo asked leading mayoral candidates for our positions on the issue just a few days before the vote.[39] Worried about appearing too radical, and well aware of Prime Minister Trudeau's refusal to consider decriminalizing drugs, I told Woo, "I don't think that it's going to come at the federal level any time soon, so I just want to focus on stuff I can accomplish. I wouldn't waste my political capital on something that's not going to happen." Sim admitted he did not know the difference between legalization and decriminalization, but preferred fining those caught with drugs. Only Sylvester got it right by stating she supported "decriminalization as part of an overall strategy" and as mayor "would work toward it in collaboration with Ottawa, the RCMP, and Vancouver police."

Fortieth Mayor of Vancouver

On October 20, 2018, my team crowded into the very budget-friendly Waldorf Hotel's iconic Tiki Bar on Hastings Street to watch the results come in. While public polling said I would win in a cakewalk, the race was much closer. As with my 2011 victory in Burnaby–Douglas and my 2015 victory in Burnaby South, I was declared elected only after the very last ballot box was opened and counted, well after midnight. With 49,705 votes, I had finished just 957 votes ahead of Ken Sim, who had support from 48,748 voters; third-place Shauna Sylvester had 35,457 votes. Holding Jeanette's hand in the air and hugging my brother, Evan, campaign manager Neil Monckton, communications director Alvin Singh, organizers Anita Zaenker and Krystal Smith, and the rest of my team, I promised the crowd I would get to work right away. I was mayor of Vancouver!

Looking back, I now understand I would never have become Vancouver mayor without Shauna Sylvester being in the race. As mentioned earlier, about fifty thousand Vancouver voters tend to support left mayoral candidates, fifty thousand support right candidates, and thirty thousand or so prefer centrist candidates. In the past, only slightly centre-left candidates, such as Gregor Robertson, and centre-right candidates, such as Philip Owen, had been able to amass enough votes to win. Candidates seen as too far to the left, like me, just lose too many centrist votes to finish first. But I was elected, as Sylvester pulled just enough centrist votes away from the centre-right Sim for me to win. Sim spent over $1 million on his campaign, compared with my $328,228, and initially refused to concede defeat.[40]

My election as mayor in 2018 was both a blessing and a curse. Although I secured the mayor's chair, I had no direct allies on council, as I had run as an independent without the backing of a civic party. My opponent Ken Sim had lost, but his NPA council candidates secured five of ten council seats— one away from a majority. The centrist Green Party won three seats, the centre-left OneCity party candidate Christine Boyle won one seat, and Jean Swanson won one seat for the radical-left COPE party. Essentially, this configuration resulted in a five-five vote split on council—five NPA councillors on the centre-right and five councillors from the centre- and far-left—meaning I needed to build coalitions on every council vote, of which there were thousands. I would side with NPA councillors to approve rental housing, while the Green Party and COPE oddly tended to vote against such proposals. I would side with the Greens, COPE and OneCity to secure redistributive and progressive social policy, while the NPA voted against tax increases, new social housing, and health measures such as overdose prevention sites. In some cases, I could encourage all councillors to support my policy proposals, but I had to pick my issues sparingly, as this approach took months of planning and campaigning.

This unusual situation of having no partisan colleagues on council, and at times ten political foes, meant that the mayor's office usually needed to operate on a stand-alone basis, despite having little formal power. Hollywood often portrays mayors as having hundreds of employees, but my office was very small. Neil Monckton became one co-chief of staff, handling all external matters, such as federal and provincial relations and outreach to community partners we needed to build housing, and was assisted by the trilingual Alex Chen. Lauren Reid, a former SFU graduate student of mine who also worked in my parliamentary office, was

Monckton's deputy chief, handling decriminalization and other tough files. Anita Zaenker came over from the labour movement to serve as my other co-chief of staff to handle all internal matters, including the unsung job of wrangling the motley crew of councillors, with Laurie MacLean serving as her senior legislative advisor. Alvin Singh was a one-person show, handling all my communications except when assisted for short periods by Simka Marshall and Akeena Legall. This was the small but highly skilled team tasked with helping the most left-leaning mayor in Vancouver's history handle everything from the pandemic to an Olympic Games bid.

My top two priorities coming out of the election were increasing the supply of affordable housing and reducing illicit drug–related deaths. In terms of housing, Vancouver has one of the most privatized housing markets in the world, with governments owning just 5 percent of the housing stock and the remaining 95 percent in the hands of private owners. This stands in marked contrast to many European and Asian cities where governments provide between 25 and 70 percent of the housing. With very little senior government investment in housing, my team focused on lobbying senior governments to provide more social housing and incentivize private-sector developers to shift from building market condominiums to building secure market rental homes. This tight focus soon began to produce real results.

I also got rolling very quickly with my overdose task force, introducing a motion to council at the first regular meeting, in November 2018. It received unanimous support, and two weeks later a powerhouse 115-person team composed of the most knowledgeable people in the city began to share their ideas as to how to move forward.[41] Staff reported their find-ings at a well-attended December 21 special council meeting, after a series of meetings with people with lived experience, sex workers, front-line service providers, police and health-care workers, many of which I personally attended in co-op and social-housing common rooms. Recommendations included expanding effective harm-reduction measures out-side the Downtown Eastside to save lives across the entire city, working with the provincial government to expand safer-supply measures, and funding new front-line, peer-led programs such as Tenant Overdose Response Organizers (TORO), where tenants in deeply affordable and social-housing buildings work with nurses to provide overdose response training and implement harm reduction measures for their neighbours—including the distribution of naloxone, a widely distributed medication that rapidly reverses an opi-oid overdose by blocking the effects of opioids in the brain.

While the City of Vancouver was going far beyond the traditional role of a municipality, spending close to $4 mil-lion per year in property-tax revenue to address the illicit drug–related death crisis, drug users and their advocates were critical of the Mayor's Overdose Emergency Task Force report. They were disappointed that it did not include stronger action to decriminalize the possession of small amounts of drugs.[42] From my perspective, I felt I had done the best I could, considering I was leading a deeply divided council, half of which had run with Ken Sim and the NPA and were looking to trip me up whenever possible. For example, NPA councillor Lisa Dominato marched into my office before our first council meeting to tell me she was going to cut my mayor's office budget in half. Dominato was unable to convince other councillors to take this action, but she and her NPA colleagues voted against every budget, insisting we should cut taxes and services to the public. I was satisfied with the task force recommendations, but knew they merely marked the beginning of my work, and that I would need to look for other opportunities to do what I could to help save lives.

Trudeau Shuts Down Decriminalization (Again)

With work on the task force recommendations under way, I began to dedicate more of my time to securing federal housing funding. This involved developing pitches to the federal housing minister for new investment. I took the lead on this file, as my experience as an MP meant I knew Ottawa very well. Vancouver city manager Sadhu Johnston was deeply skeptical I would be able to secure federal housing funding, because previous Vancouver city governments had not been able to do so, but Neil Monckton and I began contacting federal ministers in earnest to try and get an initial deal. Prime Minister Trudeau had been good enough to call me shortly after my October 20 election victory, and we had our first face-to-face meeting on November 1 in Vancouver, where we pleasantly chatted about future housing and transit investments and, of course, the TMX pipeline expansion. Nothing was settled, but I thought the meeting went well. We did not discuss illicit drug–related deaths at that first meeting.

I travelled to Ottawa in January 2019 to attend my first Federation of Canadian Municipalities Big City Mayors conference. I met with the federal NDP caucus and was chuffed by the warm welcome I received, and I also met the Liberal minister of families, children and social development, Jean-Yves Duclos, who held the federal housing portfolio. We had a productive talk in his office along with Liberal MP Adam Vaughan, a former Toronto city councillor and now parliamentary secretary to Minister Duclos. I was surprised at how open they both were to working together on the housing file, and how readily they agreed to immediately work on an initial investment deal for Vancouver. Although the learning curve was steep, I felt I was making good progress.

A decline in illicit drug–related deaths in 2019 provided hope that the measures being taken by the City, the Province of British Columbia, and Vancouver Coastal Health, such as widespread naloxone distribution and expanded overdose-prevention site services, were beginning to have a positive effect. Deaths had dropped by 40 percent from the previous year, and while the number was still terrifyingly high, it suggested we might be turning the corner. And so I continued to support Arts, Culture, and Community Services general manager Sandra Singh, Managing Director of Social Policy Mary Clare Zak, and their committed staff as they implemented our task force recommendations and continued to learn from those with lived experience and from front-line workers.

Decriminalization discussions also briefly resurfaced in British Columbia because of an April 2019 report published by Provincial Health Officer Dr. Bonnie Henry, entitled *Stopping the Harm.*[43] Dr. Henry's report offered a single recommendation: decriminalize people who use drugs. Moreover, after confirming the Trudeau government's firm refusal to decriminalize hard drugs at the federal level, Dr. Henry instead implored the province move on its own:

> In the context of the continuing overdose crisis that is affecting families and communities across BC, the province cannot wait for action at the federal level. Immediate provincial action is warranted, and I recommend that the Province of BC urgently move to decriminalize people who possess controlled substances for personal use. This is an important additional step to stem the tide of unprecedented deaths.
>
> Decriminalization of people who use drugs can be achieved through two provincial mechanisms. The first option is to use provincial legislation (specifically, the *Police Act*) that allows the Minister of Public Safety and Solicitor General to set broad provincial priorities with respect to people who use drugs. This could include declaring a public health and harm reduction approach as a provincial priority to guide law enforcement in decriminalizing and de-stigmatizing people who use drugs. This type of approach would provide pathways for police to link people to health and social services and would support the use of administrative penalties rather than criminal charges for simple possession. The second option is to develop a new regulation under the *Police Act* to include a provision that prevents

any member of a police force in BC from expending resources on the enforcement of simple possession offences under Section 4(1) of the CDSA.[44]

Stopping the Harm marked a critical milestone on the road to decriminalization. Not only did Dr. Henry state that decriminalization was an important action government could take to reduce illicit drug overdose deaths, but she also exposed for the first time that the BC provincial government could effectively decriminalize drugs under its own authority and without federal intervention. This was the moment for which so many drug policy reform advocates had been waiting—BC's top doctor was not only pleading for provincial action on behalf of grieving families, but publicly declaring it was possible for the BC government to do it right away and under its own authority.

However, any hope of reform was soundly crushed when BC minister of public safety Mike Farnworth rolled out the provincial government's response to the report:

We all agree on supporting police and first responders to connect more people to the treatment and the care that they need. However, possessing these substances is still illegal under federal law. No provincial action can change that. And as is the case with cannabis, no one province can go it alone...It's not appropriate for me as minister to be directing police on how they conduct their operations. What we need to ensure is that people are able to get the help and the treatment that they need.[45]

The federal Trudeau and provincial Horgan governments had now made it brutally clear on multiple occasions
that their governments would not decriminalize, no matter how many people died from toxic drugs. The window
of opportunity appeared slammed shut and truly shut-
tered. Most, including me, thought there was no point in
continuing to pursue decriminalization. But not all politicians were satisfied. In June 2019, in the final days of the
forty-second Parliament, backbench Liberal MP Nathaniel
Erskine-Smith introduced an explosive private member's bill.
C-460 proposed amending the federal Controlled Drugs and
Substances Act to end criminal sanctions for low-level possession of drugs. Although well-intentioned, Erskine-Smith's
last-minute effort probably did more harm than good, as he
had no ability to trigger a vote in the House of Commons, let
alone enough time to guide the bill through Parliament and
into law. C-460 garnered fierce attacks from Conservative
Party leader Andrew Scheer, who placed ads in English and
Chinese media stating, "Justin Trudeau has a plan to legalize
hard drugs!" and forcing Trudeau to continuously repeat his
pledge not to decriminalize.[46]

Back on the housing front in Vancouver, I was ecstatic
when, in August 2019, Minister Duclos said he was coming
to Vancouver to announce his government would invest
$184 million in several housing projects around the city. City
staff and the provincial government were surprised we were
able to secure this unprecedented amount of funding in less
than a year on the job, which would supply many units of
much-needed affordable housing. I was encouraged when
Prime Minister Trudeau's staff informed my office that

the prime minister was also coming to Vancouver city hall for a visit.

Before discussing the details of his visit, this is as good a place as any to explain my relationship with the prime minister. Prime ministers are critical to federal policy reform of any type, as they ultimately decide whether change will or will not occur. They approve all candidates and select all cabinet ministers. They author ministerial mandate letters to direct the proactive policies they wish implemented and have the final say on how to deal with emerging issues. They are the key players when dealing with other heads of government. Most Canadian prime ministers speak with provincial premiers, but Prime Minister Trudeau developed the rare practice of regularly speaking with mayors of Canada's largest cities—including many conversations with me that provided more insight than I ever thought I would gain as to how this country runs.

I have been in Prime Minister Trudeau's orbit since 2011, when I was elected the member of Parliament for Burnaby-Douglas. We were both assigned third-bench seats in the House of Commons by our respective parties. Where you sit in the House of Commons indicates your status within the party—believe me, everything in that place is about hierarchies. Front-benchers closest to the prime minister or leader of the official opposition have the most power within caucus. Those sitting in the very last of the five rows of seats (now six rows in the new House of Commons) are either trouble-makers or lunatics and are placed as far as possible from their leaders. Third-benchers are the MPs with whom the party does not know what to do. Too risky for the front bench. Too active for the back bench. I remember looking down the third bench in 2011 and seeing a rather bored Justin Trudeau, and saying hi a few times when we passed in the corridors. I was in the House when people started to notice Trudeau more, especially after he called Conservative environment minister Peter Kent a "piece of shit" for attacking NDP Halifax MP Megan Leslie when she criticized the Conservative government for withdrawing from the Kyoto Protocol.

Our paths did not cross often before the 2015 election, and rarely after the member of Parliament for Papineau became prime minister and the NDP fell into third-party status. I was still on the third bench, but he now had the best seat in the house. Trudeau always seemed to have much more fun than Stephen Harper did when answering questions from opposition members, and was both more sincere and more showy than his predecessor. Harper sought to survive question period, whereas Trudeau used it to build team spirit and morale. You believed Trudeau cared about people, but he did not give a fig what you thought of him. When the House of Commons cameras were off, Trudeau leisurely leaned back in his seat and looked around himself for entertainment. His laugh and knee-slapping sometimes seemed somewhat forced. In stark contrast, Harper was always head-down in his paperwork when the cameras were off and never offered a laugh in the House, not even an evil chortle.

This mindset sometimes got away from Trudeau. I remember sitting very close to NDP MP Ruth Ellen Brousseau when the prime minister angrily crossed the floor to confront NDP members who were purposely delaying House proceedings by refusing to take their seats. Some contact between members ensued and Trudeau accidentally elbowed Brousseau in the breast. It was an unsettling scene, and while the prime minister immediately apologized, I always thought he came out of it much better than Brousseau, who was an innocent victim. I remember how his caucus rallied around him, while from my bus window later that night I saw Brousseau walking away from the Parliament buildings in the dark, by herself. The masculinized culture of the institution runs deep, even with a new and apparently "feminist" Parliament.

Much of what little engagement I had with Trudeau in the House of Commons came from me placing him at the centre of a campaign I had been heading since 2012 to stop the government from permitting the TMX pipeline expansion through British Columbia. I was an unrelenting voice opposing the government permitting a new pipeline running from the Alberta tar sands to Vancouver. I raised the issue in the House every chance I got and ran hard-hitting videos specifically targeting the prime minister for forcing the new pipeline through First Nations' unceded territories. I know he noticed the campaign and did not like it. Looking back, my own experience with personalized attacks on me makes me think that on some occasions I may have gone too far.

Our relationship dramatically changed when I became mayor in 2018. Prime Minister Trudeau called me at home to congratulate me hours after my October 20 victory, then travelled to Vancouver for a sit-down meeting two weeks later. I was a bit overwhelmed by his generosity and willingness to get beyond my previous political affiliation and highly personalized anti-pipeline campaign. We met and spoke many times over my four years in office, both in person and on the phone, or in small, closed-group meetings, such as with the Federation of Canadian Municipalities Big City Mayors' Caucus. I was always struck by how open our discussions were and how he never tried to control what I said to the media after our meetings. While having frank conversations about serious issues, we always seemed to have a good laugh about things, mostly at the expense of the Conservatives.

During an August 2019 conversation at Vancouver city hall, Prime Minister Trudeau sat across from me at my board-room table and said straight to my face, "Kennedy, we are not going to decriminalize drugs." What surprised me was that his declaration was unprompted. I did not push for decrim-inalization at all during this meeting. He just came out and told me he was opposed to this reform as soon as I raised the general topic of reducing drug-related deaths. I now see that he made his blunt proactive declaration to ensure I would not make a mistake when talking to the media about the issue. I feel Trudeau opposed decriminalization because he thought the political risk was too high, especially when, unbeknownst to me during that meeting, he was just days away from calling an election. Conservative leader Andrew Scheer was a social conservative who would stop at nothing to rile up his right-leaning base and more centrist-leaning Canadians to scare them away from Liberal candidates. He was already attacking the prime minister on this subject, say-ing that Trudeau planned to legalize all drugs, which would endanger their children.

Decriminalization was not at the top of my list at that meeting anyway, partly because the rate of illicit drug–related deaths had dramatically declined in 2019, and partly because Vancouver chief medical health officer Dr. Patricia Daly had convinced me to focus more on securing additional federal help with local safer-supply programs. This seemed like good advice, as Trudeau was much more open to helping with safer supply, but still made no concrete promises. I was fine with a vague commitment. I needed to keep him onside to secure assistance on other issues, such as more housing investments and extending the Broadway subway out to the University of British Columbia. That day, I told the media I was very grateful for Trudeau's $184 million investment in affordable housing in our city, and for "really helping us reduce the deaths due to overdose with record investments here as well as legislative change."[47]

By September 2019, I was feeling pretty good about my transition from MP to mayor. I had a good relationship with the federal government, and it was starting to pay off with important housing investments. The Mayor's Overdose Emergency Task Force had been a success and the recommendations were starting to hit the ground, although decriminalizing drugs was firmly off the local, provincial and federal agenda. I felt as if my staff and I had hit a groove, and I even started thinking about serving another term. Then Trudeau rolled the dice and called an election, and the ground began to tilt in another direction.

6

THE WINDOW OPENS

THE QUEST TO DECRIMINALIZE DRUGS SEEMED HOPELESS IN September 2019. While the need was great, there was no political will to move ahead, even with important figures such as representatives of Vancouver's drug-using community, Dr. Bonnie Henry, federal NDP leader Jagmeet Singh, and a host of health professionals and policy researchers calling for change. The Trudeau government had said no. The Horgan government had said no. There was no path for me to pursue the matter at the local level, and while I had not said no, I did not have time to focus on this when I had so many other files to work on, including advancing safer supply. Yet, despite being absent from the political agenda, controlled and illicit drugs would be decriminalized in British Columbia a mere three and a half years later, mainly because new political actors emerged to play key roles in opening a window of opportunity for drug policy reform.

The 2019 Federal Election and Beyond

On September 11, 2019, Prime Minister Trudeau asked Governor General Julie Payette to dissolve Parliament and call an election for October 21. It was a strange experience, watching others campaign for federal seats while I looked on and continued my work at city hall after participating as a candidate in the previous two national contests. Drug policy played a very small role in the national election campaign. Conservative Party leader Andrew Scheer, whom I, as mayor, publicly said would be a "disaster" for Vancouver if he were to become prime minister, continued to claim Trudeau would legalize all drugs and endanger young people, and vowed to step up the war on drugs by bringing in new penalties and banning supervised consumption sites. In response, and clearly on the defensive, Trudeau responded to Scheer's attacks by saying he was "not looking at full decriminalization at all right now...There are other things that we are doing that (are) having a big impact and we're going to make decisions based on science."[48]

When the dust cleared, Trudeau remained prime minister, but lost his majority. The Liberals won twenty-seven fewer seats than they had secured in the 2015 election. Andrew Scheer's Conservatives remained official opposition and added twenty-two seats. The separatist Bloc Québécois won thirty-two seats to move past the NDP as national third party. Jagmeet Singh's party finished fourth, after losing twenty seats. I was relieved by the results, although few others seemed to agree. I thought I would have a greater ability to influence the Trudeau minority government, as I had already worked with key Liberal ministers, and the NDP caucus with which I had served for seven years now held the balance of power.

I did not want to lose any time in establishing my connections with the Liberal government and timed my next Ottawa trip to coincide with the swearing-in of the new Liberal cabinet on November 20. One advantage of spending time in the House of Commons is that once you have been elected, you need just wear your parliamentary pin to access buildings within the Parliamentary Precinct and then walk the halls to see who you can bump into without waiting for an appointment. That is exactly what I did to meet the new federal housing minister, Ahmed Hussen. I met him in the hallway outside his office literally minutes after he returned from his swearing-in ceremony and was his very first official meeting. We discussed how we could work together to build upon the almost $200 million housing investment I had secured a few months earlier. He was into it, and over the years we worked together to secure hundreds of millions of dollars in additional housing funding for Vancouver—the largest federal housing investment in the city's history.

While I was waiting to do an interview with Evan Solomon, host of the CTV television series *Power Play*, I also happened to bump into another new cabinet member: Health Minister Patty Hajdu. Minister Hajdu and I had spoken on several occasions during my attempt to pass my private member's bill, C-237, the Candidate Gender Equity Act, while I was an MP. During our chat, I said I was up for any help she might care to offer to combat illicit drug–related deaths. She was deeply sympathetic and informed me that she had worked for a long time overseeing harm-reduction service delivery in her hometown of Thunder Bay. I was so pleased that she was open to doing more, and we made an agreement to meet again soon.

Unlike her predecessor, Ginette Petitpas Taylor, Health Minister Hajdu was an expert on managing drug use and harm reduction and had worked at the Thunder Bay District Health Unit for nine years as a health promotion planner.[49] This was followed by three years coordinating the city's drug strategy and co-authoring the *Roadmap for Change* report—the vision statement of which is "to improve the health, safety and well-being of all citizens by working together to reduce the harm caused by substance use."[50] Just prior to her election in 2015, Hajdu completed her master's of public administration at the University of Victoria, submitting a major project entitled "Key Factors Contributing to Political Adoption of Municipal Drug Strategies," overseen by Donald MacPherson, the City of Vancouver's former drug policy coordinator and executive director of the Canadian Drug Policy Coalition. In her master's project, Hajdu explained that cities only adopt progressive drug strategies with the emergence of "strong political champion(s) from the beginning of the process."[51] It soon became clear that she took her own words to heart.

Upon returning to Vancouver from Ottawa, I was contacted by Deputy Prime Minister and Finance Minister Chrystia Freeland, who asked if she could fly to Vancouver to talk with me about helping her with an important issue. Freeland came to city hall on December 16, 2019, and, much to my surprise, raised the issue of free trade. The deputy prime minister had just negotiated the new Canada–United States–Mexico Agreement (CUSMA) and now had to pass the treaty through Parliament. Freeland's problem was that the Liberals no longer had a parliamentary majority and required support of one or more opposition parties to ratify the agreement in very short order. Unfortunately for Freeland, the opposition parties were still raw from their election losses and were making life difficult for the Trudeau Liberals, especially in the Standing Committee on International Trade through which CUSMA would need to quickly pass without the Liberals having enough votes to make it happen on their own within the required timeframe. It was a tense situation.

It turned out the Manitoba NDP MP Daniel Blaikie, whom I knew well, was the NDP lead on the committee. I said to Freeland in December that I would help her negotiate with Blaikie to secure the necessary NDP support but also told her I would suggest that Blaikie come up with a list of reasonable demands to which Freeland would need to agree before the NDP would support CUSMA. I called Blaikie and we talked about this being a good opportunity to do a good thing for Canada while getting concessions for working people. Blaikie agreed, and he and Freeland worked out a deal that bene-fited both parties, and CUSMA was ratified in March 2020. This was no easy feat for Blaikie, as many NDP MPs were deeply opposed to the new CUSMA, and he was required to use all his considerable skills to secure the needed votes. The very small role I had played in this adventure increased my stand-ing with the Liberals as well as my former NDP colleagues, because I had shown I could be trusted by both parties on important matters.

Looking back, 2019 was my best year as mayor. I was enjoying the work and accomplishing good things for Vancouver. I did not think things could get much better, until Prime Minister Trudeau seemed to signal in a year-end interview that he might have adjusted his hard no to decriminalizing drugs. On December 19, 2019, Trudeau said, "I was absolutely opposed to decriminalization of marijuana for many years and opposed to legalization. I am now opposed to decriminalization of hard drugs." This seemed to suggest that Trudeau might now be coming to see the criminalization of hard drugs in the same way he once viewed the criminalization of cannabis. When pushed for clarity by the reporter, Trudeau said decriminalizing hard drugs "is not something that I would be convinced is—or even could be—the panacea," insisting that other moves are "more likely to have a quicker and more significant impact in the coming years."[52] Maybe decriminalization was possible after all...

A City under Strain

The glow of 2019 immediately began to fade in the early weeks of 2020. In January, Vancouver chief constable Adam Palmer informed me Vancouver police officers had arrested and handcuffed a twelve-year-old Indigenous girl, Torianne Tweedie, and her grandfather, Maxwell Johnson, after receiving incorrect information from employees at a downtown branch of the Bank of Montreal that the two had used fake identification when applying to open a savings account for Tweedie.[53] As chair and spokesperson for the Vancouver Police Board, I issued a statement reprimanding the Bank of Montreal for providing misleading information to the police, which, in effect, saddled the bank and its employees with all the blame. I thought this was a clever way to respond to the incident while protecting myself and the police.

I immediately began to regret my choice of actions. It caused me many sleepless nights and still haunts me today. What I should have done was to immediately condemn the actions of the police and come to the defence of Johnson and Tweedie. Instead, I sided with the police, a colonial institution that continues to cause much harm to Indigenous people. My cowardice and my guilt began to drive how I viewed policing and Indigenous people, and informed all subsequent decisions, including publicly speaking out about systemic racism within the Vancouver Police Department, which was one factor that eventually caused the Vancouver Police Union to campaign against my re-election.

On the decrim file, the new health minister, Patty Hajdu, also came to Vancouver in January. Together, we toured several key health service locations, including Insite and Dr. Christy Sutherland's Molson Site, a low-barrier, peer-staffed, supervised consumption site that also pilots safer-supply programs, such as distributing liquid hydromorphone to those suffering with substance use disorders at high risk of overdose. Keen to get the new minister on the record, I organized a media scrum at the end of the tour, planting a question on decriminalization with a reporter before the event. When asked about decriminalizing drugs,

Hajdu repeated the prime minister's 2019 message that decriminalizing drugs across the country was off the table, stating, "My personal perspective on decriminalization is that it can't be done in a broad sweep...So I think that having a comprehensive kind of approach that includes things like prevention, treatment, harm reduction, enforcement, housing, those are the kind of things that are actually going to start to move the needle...It's too premature to have a conversation about full decriminalization of substances until we get to the place where we have comprehensive support for people to get well."[54]

While work on reducing illicit drug-related deaths still appeared to be on the back burner at all levels, COVID-19 reports were becoming increasingly disturbing in early 2020. By March, things were clearly going quickly downhill, but there was little guidance coming from senior governments. Canadian mayors began to speak with one another and learn from other civic leaders around the world. I remember one Zoom meeting convened by ex-Toronto mayor David Miller where an Italian mayor broke down crying when he described how municipal workers were digging and filling mass graves as the virus ripped through his unprepared city. While the Trudeau government began to consult with Canadian big-city mayors on a weekly basis to talk through options, there was little communication from the provincial government as to what we should do in Vancouver. Veteran Calgary mayor Naheed Nenshi was the first Canadian mayor to take local action, declaring a state of emergency in his city on March 15, 2020. I was extremely worried about St. Patrick's Day becoming a super-spreader event and convinced Vancouver's chief public health officer, Dr. Patricia Daly, to issue a local health order closing all bars and restaurants on March 17.

As things went from bad to worse, the province issued health orders but had not yet declared a general state of emergency, despite rising case counts. I felt I had to immediately act to avoid what I was hearing was happening in other cities around the world. When I asked Vancouver city manager Sadhu Johnston and his staff to stand with me at a media conference as I declared a local state of emergency that would empower council to take extraordinary measures to counter the virus, he flat-out refused. I was disappointed and decided to go ahead on my own, and contacted provincial NDP public safety minister Mike Farnworth to inform him of my intentions. I declared a state of emergency on Wednesday, March 18, with the provincial government declaring a province-wide state of emergency the same day.

The next few weeks were complete chaos as we struggled to meet and enforce public health orders, with my main preoccupation being securing personal protective equipment for front-line workers and ensuring we were doing everything we could to protect the over ten thousand vulnerable people living in the Downtown Eastside—many of whom were living with mental health and addiction issues. My progressive council allies were extremely helpful, but the five NPA council members continued to undermine efforts to keep the city safe by attempting to delay decisions. I rarely slept, and when I did I ground my teeth so hard I cracked a molar. I was very grateful, however, to federal ministers Kirsty Duncan and Harjit Sajjan for calling me nearly every evening to update me on the federal response, while I continued to inform them of how things were on the ground here on the West Coast.

The provincial government began to restrict daily life to counter the spread of COVID-19, in part by issuing physical distancing orders. While the orders undoubtedly saved many lives, they were a death sentence for those struggling with substance use disorder. We have 160 mostly old and dilapidated hotels here in Vancouver that we call single-room occupancy hotels (SROs), which now accommodate long-term residents in approximately 7,000 rooms, most with common bathrooms on each floor and little in the way of cooking or food storage provisions. Before COVID-19, those living in SROs were allowed to have overnight guests. This is very important to countering illicit drug–related deaths, as there is someone there to revive a resident or call for help in the case of an overdose. Plus, the guest policy puts roofs over the heads of hundreds of people who would otherwise be homeless.

When the BC provincial government mandated physical distancing orders, private and non-profit SRO operators were forced to cancel their overnight-guest policy—forcing hundreds of people onto the streets and leaving drug users to use alone. The number of people living on the street or in parks exploded, as did the illicit drug–related death rate. It was a complete nightmare. Where 248 people died from toxic drugs in Vancouver in 2019, that number spiked to 421 in 2020—a 70 percent increase. In terms of homelessness, just east of the Downtown Eastside, where most SRO hotels are located, a five-hundred-tent city sprang up in Strathcona Park, which protesters and the media dubbed Camp Kennedy Trudeau, or Camp KT for short. Local residents and activists were incensed. My right-of-centre opponents delighted in telling Vancouverites I was personally responsible for this misery and was doing nothing about it, while in reality I was working around the clock to find solutions.

To make matters worse, the City of Vancouver was facing potential fiscal peril. Most of the city's operations are paid for with residential and commercial property taxes, but a good chunk comes from user fees like parking meter revenues. With everyone staying home and not coming downtown to their offices, these fees dried up. As cities cannot run deficits, I had to work with the city management team to lay off 20 percent of our approximately eight thousand employees overnight. Worse still, I had asked a local polling firm to scientifically survey residents about the likelihood they would be able to pay their upcoming residential and commercial property taxes—and about one quarter of those responding told us they would default.[55] I went public with this information in an effort to secure bail-out funding from senior governments and was absolutely slaughtered in the media for telling the truth about our dire fiscal situation. My political opponents were even more merciless, saying I had mismanaged the city into bankruptcy. Worst of all, my chief of staff Neil Monckton's dad died of complications from COVID-19 while staying in a long-term care home, deeply affecting Neil and the whole mayor's office team. It was fucking horrible.

I struggled to lead a city collapsing under the weight of COVID-19, a failing local economy, potential insolvency, spiralling death rates, huge homeless encampments, increasing crime rates, and defiance of public health orders by individuals and businesses. Then, out of the blue, federal health minister Patty Hajdu's staff reached out to schedule a call with me. I said yes, thinking it was about COVID-19, and left it at that.

On July 9, the Canadian Association of Chiefs of Police (CACP), of which Vancouver chief constable Adam Palmer was serving as president at the time, released the final report of its Special Purpose Committee on the Decriminalization of Illicit Drugs, formed in 2018. Entitled *Decriminalization for Simple Possession of Illicit Drugs: Exploring Impacts on Public Safety and Policing*, the report offered the following conclusion:

> As the decriminalization dialogue continues to evolve and shift, the Special Purpose Committee recommends, in cooperation with the 2019 Global Studies program, that the CACP advocate for a national task force to be created which would include Public Safety, Department of Justice, the Public Prosecution Service, Health Canada, CACP representatives and subject matter experts to research Canadian drug policy reform. Specifically, reform to s. 4(1) of the *Controlled Drugs and Substances Act* related to Simple Possession and to recommend alternatives to criminal sanctions; specifically, alternatives that promote a health-based diversionary approach.[56]

While at the time of its release the report was viewed much like Dr. Bonnie Henry's 2019 recommendations to the BC provincial government, in that it was under-reported and largely ignored, the CACP document showed for the first time that police chiefs from across Canada were advocating for a fundamental change in Canadian drug policy. This report, and Chief Constable Adam Palmer's continued leadership, would prove critical to the eventual success of the efforts to decriminalize drugs in British Columbia.

Although many people in British Columbia and across Canada were waking up to rapid and devastating increases in illicit drug–related deaths, few were aware that life was being breathed back into the push to decriminalize drugs. The issue was quiet at the federal level as parliamentarians Zoomed into their House of Commons debates and neighbours nightly banged pots and pans in support of front-line health workers being crushed by the massive flood of COVID-19 admissions. However, at a July 16 media conference, BC premier John Horgan made it clear he was personally and deeply opposed to drug policy reform when he accidentally let slip his position on the illicit drug–related death crisis.

At this media conference about COVID-19 and other issues, Horgan acknowledged a record number of overdose deaths, saying the government had been doing everything it could do to address the issue inherited from the previous BC Liberal government. He also "put the federal government on notice in a very positive way" that he supported the national association of police chiefs' call to "decriminalize the personal use of opioids," declaring toxic drug deaths "a health issue" requiring "national leadership." These statements might have seemed positive to some, but they also showed that Horgan continued to view decriminalization as a policy reform for which the federal government was solely responsible, even though, a year prior, Provincial Health Officer Dr. Bonnie Henry had laid out a clear path by which the province could go it alone to save lives.

To me, Premier Horgan was deploying a classic deflection strategy where a political leader is forced to acknowledge a worsening problem that is gaining public attention but refuses to add it to their political agenda because they have not developed a deeper understanding of the issue. Or, worse, they comprehend what is happening but do not want to expend the political capital needed to address it. They then pass the burden to act to others, in this case the federal government. I know this tactic well, as I used it to avoid action on several occasions and have seen it used by others a thousand times.

Further evidence about why Premier Horgan was not acting on Dr. Henry's or the Canadian police chiefs' advice came in his response to reporters' questions at the July 16 event. CBC reporter Tanya Fletcher pointed out to the premier that 176 British Columbians had died of COVID-19 in the first six months of 2020, but that 176 British Columbians had died from poisoned drugs in the last month alone. Fletcher then asked Premier Horgan, "How do you reconcile the province's differing responses to those who are criticizing that the overdose crisis is being overshadowed by the pandemic?" Horgan's response is worth reading carefully, as it displays how this question undermined his deflection strategy (emphasis added):

I just think that these are two separate things. We have an insidious virus that affects anyone at any time, and we have an opioid crisis that involves people using drugs. Those are *choices*, initially, and then they become dependencies. So once people make those choices, they are no longer in a position to stop making those choices without medical intervention. So, I think they're two completely different things. The fact that the numbers are similar is a coincidence, but I don't believe there's anything we can learn from that. The COVID-19 crisis is a global crisis; we already see in the United States what happens if you don't follow basic guidelines...if you can't do that, those are conscious decisions people can make to protect themselves. When you're addicted to opioids, you're not making conscious decisions other than getting your next opioid. And those are issues that we need to intervene in and we're doing our level best in a very difficult time and the numbers are putting us back, no question, but there's a bunch of compelling reasons for that. The safe drug supply is not a safe drug supply, and we need to take steps to address, and those are issues I want to raise with the federal government. *We need federal intervention on the legal components of this in terms of decriminalization and we also need a national plan, because although British Columbia is hit hard by this we're not the only ones in the country.*

This response made it clear that Premier Horgan had not internalized the issue of illicit drug–related deaths and was not prepared to take actions beyond what his government was already doing. Instead, he tried to duck the issue by blaming the federal government for inaction, despite knowing there were avenues he could independently pursue without federal assistance—including safer supply and decriminalization. This was confirmed by Dr. Henry in a 2023 interview where she stated that her 2019 call for decriminalization was "dismissed by government."[57]

I had never spoken to Premier John Horgan about this issue. Frankly, I seldom had the opportunity to speak with him about any issue, as he simply refused to reply to my team's repeated meeting requests throughout my term as mayor. I can only speculate that this had to do with a personal grudge he had against me from my time as an MP. I had met John Horgan on many occasions over the years at various NDP functions, but our first official interaction in 2012 was very unpleasant. After Jack Layton tragically passed away, interim NDP national leader Nycole Turmel appointed me associate critic for natural resources with a focus on pipelines. At that point, the federal NDP had no official position on the TMX oil pipeline expansion, which was still in the early planning and approval stages. Breaking with the party's general silence on TMX, I began to publicly oppose the new pipeline after speaking at length with Tsleil-Waututh Chief Leah George-Wilson and my constituents. My brother, Evan, worked for the Tsleil-Waututh Nation, in whose unceded territories my constituency was located.

I was immediately hauled into Turmel's office when the media began to report my opposition to the project. Chief of Staff Anne McGrath, of whom I am still very fond, told me the federal NDP could not oppose TMX because it was supported by the BC New Democratic Party led by Adrian Dix, with John Horgan serving as official opposition critic for energy. McGrath set up a call with Horgan and other BC and federal NDP party officials. The discussion was shorter than I had anticipated, as Horgan told me to "fuck off" and slammed the phone down not far into the conversation. Not a great start.

Our relationship did not improve when I became mayor in 2018. I was under the wrong impression that an NDP mayor and an NDP premier would work together. I suspect Premier Horgan had not dropped his grudge against me on the TMX file, and I also retroactively discovered I had greatly angered him when I decided early in my mayoral mandate to support newly elected centre-right Surrey mayor Doug McCallum's commitment to change a new rapid transit line running through his city from light rail to much more expensive SkyTrain technology. The change required a vote at the regional TransLink Mayors' Council, which later passed only because of my support. Apparently, Premier Horgan was furious and continued his silent treatment, even during the pandemic. I can count on one hand the number of times we discussed city business on the phone or in person—even at the height of COVID-19, when the city so desperately needed provincial support. My perception is that Horgan, like many, had not come to fully realize the extreme gravity of the poisoned drug crisis, nor was he willing to invest the political capital needed to reduce deaths. My read on one of his decisions is that Horgan created the Ministry of State for Mental Health and Addictions to use as a shield to protect his minister of health from having to directly deal with the massive increase in toxic drug deaths, but he did not provide those holding this new minister of state position with the power or resources to tackle the largest killer of young people in the province. Horgan simply did not see illicit drug–related deaths as his problem to solve.

Meanwhile, as with most folks, things were going horribly for me and my staff—working from home, spending hours in online council meetings and public hearings where councillors continued to act on whatever spur-of-the-moment whims they had, including, for example, voting not to hire a new fire chief. I eventually persuaded them to reverse this decision, after pleading it was essential for us to have a fire chief in the middle of two public health emergencies. Then, in July, just when council began its annual summer break, Health Minister Patty Hajdu contacted me to talk about the now escalating toxic drug crisis:

Minister Hajdu: *Kennedy, I've had my staff look into it and it is legally possible for Vancouver to go it alone and decriminalize drugs within the city limits. Would you be willing to do this?*

Me: *Yes. When do we start?*

7

THE WINDOW CLOSES

THE PERIOD BETWEEN AUGUST 2020 AND AUGUST 2021 IS A blur. The COVID-19 virus and measures taken to protect the public continued to radically impact the city. While municipalities could immediately feel these effects on the ground, the federal and provincial governments were somewhat slower in responding. When relief did come, in the form of direct federal funding to cities, it fell upon our exhausted council and city staff to turn federal dollars into facilities and services. Although vaccines miraculously began to roll out in late 2020 and early 2021, cities everywhere were still under enormous pressures, and illicit drug–related deaths continued to spiral out of control in Vancouver and elsewhere. Those opposed to COVID-19 public health measures and vaccine mandates began to organize and push back against front-line health workers and those charged with enforcing public health orders. During these enormous challenges, I continued to work with Minster Hajdu to move ahead with decriminalizing drugs in the city of Vancouver, with great hope that something good might come out of the all-encompassing disaster facing our city.

Cracks in the Foundation

I had enjoyed strong public support until the summer of 2020, but the city was becoming increasingly hard to manage, especially as an independent mayor with one vote on council, up against five centre-right NPA councillors and an increasingly polarized council. By August, we had five hundred tents in Strathcona Park and other temporary shelters springing up across the city. We also had an empty downtown, which prompted business closures and a corresponding increase in property crime. Drug-related deaths had climbed to one per day. These were deep and systemic problems with no easy fix, but it was hard to convey this information to a beleaguered and increasingly impatient public and media. I also had internal problems, as my city manager, Sadhu Johnston, announced he would resign at the end of 2020 because of increasing tension between him and councillors. My head planner, Gil Kelley, also resigned a few months later, and I was still looking for a new fire chief.

My political opponents, especially the NPA city councillors who ran with Ken Sim in 2018, exploited the situation by joining in a concerted campaign to blame me for the negative COVID-19–related changes in Vancouver, rather than pursuing an all-hands-on-deck approach to dealing with the intersecting crises. The media hungrily piled on as well. One local reporter worked with opponents of mine who paid a struggling couple to set up a tent so as to block entry to the condo building where Jeanette and I rent, to generate a gotcha-style news story when city staff asked the couple to relocate across the street. My approval ratings began to drop. Sensing opportunity, Ken Sim announced he would again stand for mayor in the 2022 election.

With little support within the city, and with the province not returning calls for help, my strongest ally remained the Trudeau cabinet. By working together, we were assembling a massive deal to acquire homes for those living in tents in Strathcona Park. Our strategy was to persuade campers to voluntarily move into new accommodations, rather than have police clear the park and simply force those living in the worst possible circumstances, now including families with kids, into even worse situations. I always viewed court injunctions and police-led encampment clearances as inhumane and fought against them my entire time at city hall. In the weak, weak mayor system in which I worked, only the Vancouver Board of Parks and Recreation had the legal authority to apply for court-ordered park clearances, and park board commissioners were reluctant to take these steps. Most park board officials and I agreed that only the federal and provincial governments had the resources needed to house those in the most desperate need, but at this stage the premier and his cabinet seemed reluctant to provide the necessary supports to get people inside. And then Premier Horgan decided to go to the polls.

From Talk to Action

Vancouver city council resumed sitting on September 15, 2020, and a week later Premier Horgan called a snap election. This affected the city's ability to coordinate any new actions with the provincial government as Horgan campaigned against inept BC Liberal Party leader Andrew Wilkinson to control the province. There was very little discussion of Vancouver issues during the election, with most debate centred on whether the election should have been called in the first place. When the smoke cleared on October 20, Premier Horgan had secured the NDP's long-sought majority government. Horgan appointed his new cabinet a month later, with the biggest change for Vancouver being MLA David Eby remaining as attorney general but assuming the added portfolio of minister of housing. Finally, someone in the provincial government with whom I could work on housing!

While the premier was appointing his cabinet and drafting the ministerial letters outlining their assigned goals and objectives, the drive to decriminalize drugs was moving ahead on various fronts. First, on November 3, 2020, 58 percent of Oregon voters passed Measure 110—the Drug Decriminalization and Addiction Treatment Initiative.[58] The measure instructed the state legislature to make "personal non-commercial possession of a controlled substance no more than a Class E violation (maximum fine of $100)" and to establish "a drug addiction treatment and recovery program funded in part by the state's marijuana tax revenue and state prison savings." This was an extraordinary step forward for a

US state and a very different approach to drug policy reform than that followed in Canada.[59] The approval of Measure 110 began to shift the dialogue around drug policy, especially on the West Coast of the US and Canada.

On November 17, with the provincial election behind us, I gave Vancouver city council formal notice that I would submit a motion seeking their support to decriminalize drugs in the city of Vancouver. Motion B.4, Work with Senior Governments to Address the Overdose Crisis, was debated and unanimously passed at the November 25 Standing Committee meeting. By approving my motion, council authorized me to request a federal exemption from the Controlled Drugs and Substances Act to decriminalize personal possession of illicit substances within the city's boundaries for medical purposes, to address urgent public health concerns caused by the overdose crisis and COVID-19. It was an extraordinary moment, but while past drug-policy reform efforts in the city, such as the needle exchange, four-pillar drug policy, and supervised consumption site, had generated mountains of media coverage and feature-length movies, my tweet announcing that the motion had successfully passed received a mere 32 comments and 192 likes on Twitter—a clear sign of an exhausted and frustrated public.

Vancouver city council authorized me to lead a particular scope of work on behalf of the Corporation of the City of Vancouver by passing this formal motion. Under the Controlled Drugs and Substances Act, those found guilty of possessing any amount of heroin, cocaine, opium, fentanyl, morphine, methamphetamines or other "Schedule 1" drug have criminal records and are subject to a first-offence fine not exceeding $1,000 or imprisonment of up to six months, or both. A second offence can bring a fine not exceeding $2,000, up to one year in prison, or both, with courts authorized to imprison offenders for no more than seven years under certain conditions. However, the federal minister of health has been delegated broad discretion under Section 56 of the CDSA:

> The Minister may, on any terms and conditions that the Minister considers necessary, exempt from the application of all or any of the provisions of this Act or the regulations any person or class of persons or any controlled substance or precursor or any class of either of them if, in the opinion of the Minister, the exemption is necessary for a medical or scientific purpose or is otherwise in the public interest.[60]

In other words, with a simple stroke of the pen, and without the formal permission of Parliament or even the prime minister, the federal minister of health can waive these criminal sanctions for drug possession under their own delegated authority. The health minister does not have the authority under the CDSA to legalize—that is, to allow the legal production, sale and possession of—a scheduled drug. That would require a change in the law, which would need to pass through the House of Commons and Senate, and receive royal assent. However, federal health ministers have the authority to decriminalize a scheduled drug—that is, to suspend criminal sanction under certain conditions that they decide under their authority.

Statistics Canada recorded 61,798 police-reported possession, trafficking, production and importation or exportation
offences in 2021 in Canada, which included offences under
the Controlled Drugs and Substances Act and the Cannabis
Act.[61] Police reported 17,880 offences in British Columbia
in 2021, of which over 8,000 were related to heroin, cocaine,
methamphetamine, opioids or ecstasy, most of which would
be related to mere drug possession.[62] Vancouver varied from
the national norm when it came to arresting people for possessing small amounts of hard drugs, with the Vancouver
Police Department having recommended that fewer than five
hundred people be charged with possession between 2011
and 2020. However, and importantly, the VPD was making
thousands of drug seizures per year, forcing those with substance use disorders to undertake risky and often criminal
behaviour to replace the drugs seized by police.[63]

The City of Vancouver would now apply to federal health
minister Hajdu to exempt all those within the boundaries
of the city from criminal sanctions for the simple possession of certain hard drugs. Seen from this perspective, the
organization most affected by decriminalization would
be the Vancouver Police Department, as police would no
longer have the authority or responsibility to arrest those
caught possessing drugs, or to even seize these drugs.
Decriminalizing drugs in the city of Vancouver would require
determining which drugs were to be exempt from the CDSA
sanctions and, importantly, how much of the drug or drugs
someone could be caught carrying before criminal sanctions
would apply. It was up to the City of Vancouver team to do
the hard work of determining these crucial components of

our application, which Health Minister Hajdu and her Health Canada team would then evaluate before deciding whether to grant the City of Vancouver a CDSA exemption. I also thought it important to secure as much community support for our application as I could get, especially from local First Nations, as the Section 56 exemption would also apply to the unceded territories on which Vancouver is located, as well as to Musqueam and Squamish reserve lands.

On top of these challenges, I was very aware that our Ottawa champion, federal health minister Patty Hajdu, might have a very short window in which to approve our application, as the Liberal minority government could fall at any time. I was also concerned the minister was contradicting the express wishes of Prime Minister Trudeau, who had twice told me he would never decriminalize drugs. Hajdu was also tremendously busy, as she was heading the national health response to COVID-19.

To further complicate the matter, on November 26, the day after city council approved my motion to apply to decriminalize drugs within City of Vancouver boundaries, Premier Horgan issued a formal letter to the new minister of mental health and addictions, Sheila Malcolmson, a former federal NDP member of Parliament and colleague of mine from Ottawa.[64] The letter instructed Malcolmson to work with other provincial ministers to "fast track the move toward decriminalization by working with police chiefs to push Ottawa to decriminalize simple possession of small amounts of illicit drugs for personal use. In the absence of prompt federal action, develop a made-in-BC solution that will help save lives." The letter further entrenched Premier

Horgan's declaration that while he supported the Canadian Association of Chiefs of Police's call for decriminalization, he insisted such efforts required a nationwide response from the federal government, not BC acting alone. It was heartening that Horgan now at least acknowledged Dr. Bonnie Henry's advice for the province of BC to take unilateral action, but I was still under the strong impression that this was all a bluff on behalf of the province.

Thinking the federal window for change might slam shut at any moment, and skeptical of Premier Horgan's willingness to move forward with decriminalization at the provincial level, I pushed hard to get city staff moving on my approved council motion as soon as possible. But City Manager Johnston was transitioning out, senior staff were exhausted from the pandemic, and we were amid a very contentious December 2020 civic budget. Gripped by the urgent need to move, I took the unusual step of contacting Professor Kora DeBeck, a colleague of mine at Simon Fraser University's School of Public Policy, to ask whether she would be willing to head the initial work on the federal application directly from the mayor's office.

To my great relief, Professor DeBeck agreed to join my team as a consultant in December. A Simon Fraser University associate professor and research scientist with the BC Centre on Substance Use, DeBeck specializes in evaluating health and policy interventions to reduce health and social harms among people who use drugs, with a particular focus on the prevention of high-risk substance use. DeBeck would work directly with Lauren Reid from my office, who holds an SFU master's degree in public policy, specializing in improving the lives of sex workers. Deputy Chief of Staff Reid also has significant experience in getting things done in Ottawa and liaising with community groups, after working for seven years in my member of Parliament office. I had the utmost confidence these two people would deliver, with DeBeck writing policy and Reid coordinating the approval effort.

The work began right away, with Reid heading a working group coordinated through my office that included City of Vancouver intergovernmental-relations staff led by Tobin Postma, Inspector Phil Heard from the Vancouver Police Department, and Vancouver Coastal Health director of strategic initiatives and public health planning Chris Van Veen. This team did amazing work and established the foundation of what would eventually become the official City of Vancouver application. In January 2021, Health Minister Hajdu gave us the official go-ahead to prepare our submission, setting a March 1 deadline. In a private January 26 text to me, she stated her department was "well supported to work fast." When I thanked her for her work on this file in spite of all the rest she was dealing with, the minister quoted a famous line from the late NDP leader Jack Layton, texting, "Don't let anyone tell you it can't be done." She also texted, "We will get this done if it is the last thing I do. Hopefully not the last thing, to be clear!" This revealed to me the huge political risk she was taking. Appreciative, I replied, "I'm all in!"

That Minister Hajdu had green-lighted the City of Vancouver and set a deadline of March 1 unintentionally threw the BC provincial government off-balance.[65] On February 3, the province was forced to stop hiding behind the strategy of calling for the federal government to decriminalize drugs nationwide, and, instead, pivoted to submitting its own request to decriminalize drugs province-wide. I found out that the province was moving ahead with its own decriminalization application on the same day as everyone else, as they had not given me a heads-up. However, I was determined to continue with our own submission, as I simply did not believe this was anything more than another delay tactic by the province, and we already had a sound draft submission almost ready for Health Canada to review.

The provincial application caused considerable problems for Health Minister Hajdu, who now had to decide whether to approve the City of Vancouver's application, the Province of British Columbia's application, both, or neither. I texted Minister Hajdu in early February, saying I thought the provincial application for decriminalization was "a bluff on their part." As Health Canada had officially invited us to reply and we were well under way and would not withdraw from the process, the minister would have to receive and adjudicate our application and eventually send us an official yes or no letter. We had got in just under the wire and were not going to back out.

The locus of the work on the City of Vancouver application changed in early 2021, when Deputy City Manager Paul Mochrie took over as interim city manager and veteran health-policy consultant Ted Bruce was hired to oversee the official city submission. Mochrie expanded the working group, and we consolidated the mayor's office work into the larger process led by civil servants, with Kora DeBeck moving to advise the larger team and Lauren Reid serving as the main liaison with my office. This work included continuing to consult with the community and developing a "Vancouver Model" of decriminalization.

Health officials, police, policy advisors and drug-user advocates all agreed we should pursue a purely medical model, meaning that, unlike in Oregon, those caught possessing small quantities of illicit drugs would not be ticketed by police. We also came to rapid agreement on which drugs should be included in the application to Health Canada. However, there were deep divisions over the "carry threshold"—that is, the amount of illicit drugs a person could possess without being criminally charged. Some drug-user advocates sought thresholds nearly twenty times higher than those supported by police, with health researchers somewhere in the middle of the two groups.

The increasing hostility of drug users and their advocates, along with the Province of British Columbia's decision to move forward with its own submission, was making things even tougher for Health Minister Hajdu, who, in my opinion, had already jeopardized her cabinet seat by allowing the City of Vancouver to apply for decriminalization. Minister Hajdu began to try and coordinate the city and provincial submissions, suggesting we release a joint federal, provincial and municipal statement to this effect.

On March 1, 2021, the City of Vancouver sent a preliminary submission to Health Canada to establish a working framework for the final exemption application.[66] The proposed "Vancouver Model" would set personal carry-threshold amounts, and would make referrals to addiction and health services voluntary and free of ticketing by police. Health Canada received the application and green-lighted our work to move forward. I texted Minister Hajdu after a March 4 in-person meeting, suggesting we issue a joint statement that the City's application would be all wrapped up by May. She replied that it was very important to synchronize with the province, if possible. I was very reluctant, and thinking of my past dealings with the province, I replied, "I've been tricked too many times by these guys so am suspicious." She replied, "I know—I promise I am serious, but let's try this way and see. I am with you!" In the end, these discussions did not really matter, as the province would not agree to a joint statement from all three levels of government, so I continued pushing ahead with the City of Vancouver's own submission. On April 8, the city team submitted our draft application to Health Canada, including the proposed carry-threshold levels. Based on evidence from health policy researchers, police and other experts, the City of Vancouver proposed residents be allowed to carry a three-day supply of drugs, including 2 grams of opioids (heroin, fentanyl and other powdered street opioids), or 3 grams of cocaine, or 1 gram (10 rocks) of crack cocaine, or 1.5 grams of methamphetamine. These recommended carry thresholds represented a starting point, with the expectation they would increase as the effect of the new policy was assessed. Health Canada sent a list of questions upon receiving and reviewing the draft policy, and stated we needed to respond before they would accept our final submission for the minister's consideration in mid-May.

All hell broke loose when the city team went back to consult with affected community groups regarding which drugs were to be included and at what carry thresholds. On May 3, the Vancouver Area Network of Drug Users publicly stated that "our blood will be on your hands" if we did not radically adjust the carry thresholds, claiming the Vancouver Model was devised to arm police with new tools to harm drug users and would go down in history as a deadly failure of public policy.[67] On May 10, VANDU issued a further statement resigning from the City of Vancouver's Decriminalization Working Group, saying my commitment to working with drug users "was a lie to score petty political points ahead of the electoral cycle." Many groups, including the BC Centre on Substance Use and most peer-run drug policy reform advocacy groups, wrote to Minister Hajdu, stating if the Vancouver Model was not immediately stopped, the City of Vancouver and Health Canada would "set a deadly precedent for public policy; not only in Vancouver, but across Canada and beyond."[68]

The extreme backlash endangered the entire endeavour. On many occasions, I explained to drug user advocates that the success of the application depended on maintaining the support of the Vancouver Police Department, and that the VPD would withdraw its support and sink the application if carry thresholds increased. I remember asking one prominent health policy researcher from UBC on a Zoom call if he would rather move ahead with the current, imperfect application for decriminalization or wait ten years for the next window of opportunity to open. He said, without batting an eye, that he would rather wait another ten years, which revealed to me just how disconnected academics sometimes are from reality. Here we were, with the only opportunity in the history of the country to decriminalize drugs, a precarious opportunity with very little chance of success unless we all tried, and here was a community leader willing to throw it all away, perhaps forever, because it did not fit his definition of what was perfect. Academics really are their own worst enemies sometimes.

We moved ahead despite a protest march by drug users and negative media stories, submitting our final proposal on May 28, along with letters of support and an implementation plan. Some of us worried that if we included only opioids, cocaine and methamphetamine in the proposal, those using party drugs like ecstasy might shift their casual habits to more dangerous drugs. For this reason, we included a much longer list of substances with carry thresholds, including Dilaudid (2 grams), Kadian (7.5 grams), M-Eslon (7.5 grams), oxycodone (2 grams); methadone liquid (1 gram); Suboxone (120 milligrams), clonazepam (80 milligrams), diazepam (400 milligrams), Ativan (80 milligrams), prescription stimulants (500 milligrams), MDMA (2 grams), LSD (30 units), psilocybin mushrooms (20 grams), ketamine (3 grams) and GHB (5 grams).

Minister Hajdu texted me in early June, stating that officials had informed her our application was in very good shape and that she was trying to get it approved before Parliament rose for the summer at the end of the month. On June 11, the Expert Task Force on Substance Use appointed by Minister Hajdu submitted its final report to Health Canada. Formed in March 2021 and co-chaired by Thunderbird Partnership Foundation executive director Carol Hopkins, University of Toronto professor of psychiatry Dr. Kwame McKenzie, and Abbotsford, BC, police department chief constable Mike Serr, the task force called for "a paradigm shift in policy." More specifically, the top task-force recommendation was for Health Canada to "end criminal penalties related to simple possession and...all coercive measures related to simple possession and consumption."[69] While cabinet and MPs undoubtedly saw the report, I was not aware it had been published, nor, amazingly, were media, as the report received little or no coverage.

On June 23, the last day of the parliamentary session and perhaps of the Trudeau minority government, I texted Minister Hajdu to ask if there was anything else I could do. She replied that she was trying to get the province comfortable with acknowledging the City of Vancouver's application as a "pilot" that could immediately get under way while the BC provincial government completed its own application, which was a full year behind ours. Two days later, BC minister of mental health and addictions Sheila Malcolmson called me to say the province had sent an official letter to Minister Hajdu, stating that the province did not support the City of Vancouver's decriminalization application. This reinforced my opinion that the Horgan government was not serious about decriminalizing drugs, and would try to kill the City of Vancouver application and then drag their feet on their own effort—perhaps forever. I was so relieved when Health Canada contacted us to say it was continuing to review our work, as the province had not yet submitted an application for them to consider.

In July, I texted Minister Hajdu to say we were ready to go out with a request for proposal to hire a team to come in and help City of Vancouver staff to implement our decriminalization plan, once approved. Our staff was continuing to work with Health Canada officials to iron out the exemption details. Although we had now answered all their questions, in August Health Canada officials asked whether we would raise our drug carry thresholds. I felt we should give it a try and see if the Health Canada request would help move the police to support increased limits. Staff quickly rewrote the proposal and brought it back to the working group for consideration. The Vancouver police representatives felt blindsided and said they would continue to support the City's application only if their objections to the higher limits were included in the final report to Health Canada, an inclusion that would make it politically impossible for the health minister to sign off as, in my opinion, there was no way Prime Minister Trudeau would have allowed her to stay in her job if she approved a decriminalization application from the City of Vancouver that did not have the support of the BC provincial government or Vancouver police. After working to pull everything back from the brink, on August 8, I texted the minister to say that we would proceed with our original carry thresholds to maintain police support.

There were very strong rumours that Trudeau was set to call another election, and I was terrified that people would soon go to the polls and all this effort would be for nothing. I texted Minister Hajdu on August 11:

> Hi there. We are sitting on pins and needles wondering if you are going to grant our decrim exemption before the election is called. We've done everything requested by Ministry staff—including having police and local health officials on board with our exemption

application. I don't want to be a pain but would really like to know if you are going to give us the green light. We still have one person a day dying here, and many folks are counting on us to take bold action on this critical issue. If you OK this, we'll get right to work with implementing. The province has misled both of us all the way along in this process and I don't think there is any chance they will ever implement this policy. I feel Vancouver's application is the only hope we have in exploring whether decriminalizing drugs will save lives here and across the country. Thanks for your work on this file. I very much hope we can take this step and work together to save lives of the most vulnerable. Best wishes, Kennedy.

Hajdu texted back to say she was still waiting for Health Canada officials to submit their final recommendations to the minister, which she needed to take to cabinet and discuss with her colleagues. On August 15, Prime Minister Trudeau dissolved Parliament and called an election for September 20. As I had feared, the window slammed shut on decriminalizing drugs in Vancouver, possibly forever.

8

THE WINDOW REOPENS

O UR TEAM WAS DISHEARTENED BY THE FEDERAL ELECTION being called before our decriminalization application was approved. Despite some brutal opposition along the way, we had got it to the threshold, only to have the window close in our face. All we could do was wait until the votes were counted and a new federal government formed. There was so much that could now go wrong, but there was still a slim chance our application would be approved. If the Liberals returned to government on September 20. If Patty Hajdu remained health minister. If I could hold things together on my side. I could also see my own October 2022 re-election bid on the horizon, as my opposition continued to increase their attacks. Soon I would also need to focus on returning as mayor for a second term.

The September 20, 2021, federal election initially changed very little in Ottawa, with Prime Minister Trudeau remaining in power with his second consecutive minority government. Again, no one was happy. Trudeau had failed to gain his majority. Conservative Party leader Erin O'Toole had failed to displace Trudeau, despite his efforts to move the Conservatives closer to the centre of the political spectrum on some issues. The Bloc Québécois remained the third party, with Jagmeet Singh's NDP gaining only a single new seat to remain the fourth-place party. On election night, I texted congratulations to Patty Hajdu, who would remain health minister at least until Trudeau selected his new cabinet. She texted back the next day: "Yay. Now let's get stuff done. Talk soon."

I heard nothing back from Ottawa for another month, but in the meantime, Premier Horgan started a new push to get decriminalization off the agenda. His government had indicated to Health Canada that they would request a Section 56 exemption, but they had not yet officially applied to decriminalize the possession of small amounts of drugs in the province, and, I feel, viewed the post–federal election period as the perfect time to try to change the channel. In an October 23 interview with the *Vancouver Sun* newspaper, Horgan insisted the provincial government had made repeated overtures to the federal government to start decriminalizing simple possession of opioids, but that "we have run into resistance on that front."[70] I knew this was absolute bullshit. I sent Minister Hajdu the article on October 24, and she replied, "That's ridiculous and you and I know it and it will be said one way or another." The last words Patty Hajdu ever texted me in her role as federal health minister were "Onwards friend. I'll be in touch next week. And thank you for your support."

Two days later, Prime Minister Trudeau appointed Jean-Yves Duclos to replace Patty Hajdu as minister of health, with

Dr. Carolyn Bennett appointed to a new cabinet position of minister of mental health and addictions. My main ally in this entire process could no longer help. I texted congratulations to Minister Hajdu on her appointment as minister of Indigenous services and offered to help in any way I could with her new file: "The underhanded stuff by the province is distressing and the worst kind of politics as it hurts those who need the most help. Please put in a good word for me with Duclos and Bennett and I hope to see you again soon. Kennedy."

I am of the strong opinion that Patty Hajdu's championing of drug decriminalization contributed to the prime minister shifting her from health minister to her new portfolio. We had almost got it done during her time in cabinet, but provincial government interference had kicked up enough dust to delay approval. However, there was one problem for the province and new federal ministers. The City of Vancouver's application for a Section 56 exemption had been officially received for consideration and sat on Minister Bennett's desk awaiting a response. They simply could not ignore it and have it go away. I was still hanging on by my fingernails.

I knew ministers Duclos and Bennett from my time in Ottawa as an MP. I had very little interaction with Jean Yves-Duclos when he served as minister of families, children and social development while I was sitting as a member of the NDP opposition between 2015 and 2018. However, I had contacted him upon becoming mayor in 2018, as he also had responsibility for housing and the Canadian Mortgage and Housing Corporation. We worked well together during his short tenure to bring the initial $184 million in federal social housing investment announced in Vancouver in August 2019. Through these negotiations I discovered that Minister Duclos also had a PhD in economics from the London School of Economics, which instantly connected us, as I had a PhD in government from the LSE.

I was more familiar with Minister Bennett, as I had served in the House of Commons with her between 2011 and 2018. I knew she had been a family physician for twenty years before entering politics and would view substance use disorder as a serious health issue that should not be criminalized. In 2015, when she was appointed minister of Indigenous and northern affairs, Bennett had the unenviable job of defending the Trudeau government's Reconciliation efforts as they struggled to move forward from Harper-era policies. Minister Bennett was harshly criticized on a regular basis in question period, especially by my NDP colleague Charlie Angus, who is as tough as they come. While the Trudeau government did make some progress on this very difficult file, their words about Reconciliation never quite matched their actions. Considering the immense damage caused by the continuing legacy of the Canadian Indigenous Genocide, perhaps no government could in such a short time.

Minister Bennett had only three options regarding decriminalization: officially reject the City of Vancouver's decriminalization application, approve the City of Vancouver's decriminalization application, or approve a yet-to-be-submitted application from the province of British Columbia. From where I sat, I did not believe the Horgan government wanted decriminalization, but there was no way for Bennett to quietly back out of making a public decision as long as the City of Vancouver refused to withdraw its application. To reject the City of Vancouver's application would mean that the federal government, which I felt was at least sympathetic to the policy change, as were Liberal Party members, would shoulder the entire political cost of rejecting our application, while Horgan would bear none of the political costs.

Then the province blinked. On November 1, 2021, the Province of British Columbia announced it was formally asking the federal minister of health and minister of mental health and addictions to "exercise their authority under Section 56(1) of the CDSA to exempt all persons in British Columbia 19 years of age or older from the application of Section 4(1) on the condition that the amount of any controlled substance in their possession does not exceed the thresholds for 'personal possession' set out in a Schedule."[71] The application package, which had been authored by many of the same experts who had worked on the City of Vancouver's decriminalization application, including Kora DeBeck, entered the iterative federal approval process by proposing a cumulative illicit-drug carry threshold of 4.5 grams for opioids (including heroin and fentanyl), powdered cocaine, crack cocaine and methamphetamine. In addition, the provincial model also followed the Vancouver Model to "exclude sanctions and penalties such as fines, seizure of documents, or mandatory referral to education or treatment."[72]

I could not believe that the province had moved ahead with its own decriminalization application, given Premier Horgan's consistent opposition and negative comments just a few days before. I was very happy we finally had some movement on the provincial front, and, more importantly, that the province sought to increase the cumulative carry threshold to 4.5 grams. However, I was still suspicious of their sincerity. After all, it was still possible to apply while requesting exemption conditions to which the federal government could not agree—a Shakespearean poisoned-chalice strategy where the federal government would be forced to reject a non-approvable provincial application and, subsequently, take all the blame.

Denunciations of the rushed provincial application came thick and fast. Decriminalization advocates, including the BC Association of Aboriginal Friendship Centres, the BC Centre on Substance Use, the BC/Yukon Association of Drug War Survivors, the Canadian Drug Policy Coalition, Métis Nation BC, Moms Stop the Harm, Pivot Legal Society, the Rural Empowered Drug Users Network, the Society of Living Intravenous Drug Users, and the Vancouver Area Network of Drug Users, wrote in a joint statement that while the application "marks a step in the right direction, a close read of the fine print raises concerns that the model will not adequately protect people who use drugs."[73] The province also lost the critically important backing of police when the BC Association of Chiefs of Police issued a statement declaring that it "does not support the recommendations to decriminalize 4.5 grams of illicit drugs for personal use."[74] The trap was laid: while the federal government could more or less ignore drug user advocates, it would never approve an exemption to which the police were opposed.

Ministers Duclos and Bennett reached out to me shortly after the province submitted its application, to discuss the

City of Vancouver's decriminalization application. We met in my boardroom on November 18—Minister Duclos attending by Zoom, but Minister Bennett sitting in exactly the same seat where Prime Minister Trudeau had sat a few years earlier, when he had told me that he would never decriminalize drugs. A Ministry of Health senior official and my deputy chief of staff Lauren Reid were also in attendance. After some introductory chit-chat, Minister Duclos signed off after making it clear that Minister Bennett had complete authority over the decriminalization file. We got down to brass tacks and had a frank and open discussion, which I very much appreciated. I told the minister about the weekly email to my office reporting the death count, and about the toll this was taking on the drug user community and first responders. I told her about how a member of my own family had died and how another of my relatives risked death every day. I reiterated that our application had unanimous support from city council, the three host First Nations and the Vancouver Police Department.

I grew worried, as she appeared to be unmoved but still intently listening. She said that as far as she knew, very few people had been arrested or charged for possessing drugs in the City of Vancouver in many years. If that was the case, she said, why did we need decriminalization? Then I told her what I had learned from talking with drug users and their advocates. Decriminalization was important to them, as it would mean the police would cease seizing their drugs when they were stopped either for no reason or for an unrelated incident. Ending drug seizures would subsequently reduce increased risky behaviours as drug users scrambled to replace their lost doses. I told the minister that drug users had explained to me how decriminalization would also reduce stigmatization, which would help them at home and in public, and reduce their interactions with police, which often involved harassment or violence.

I asked Minister Bennett to picture a sex worker with substance use disorder who needs to take drugs ten times per day. When stopped by police, the sex worker is found with drugs on their person, and while they are not arrested or charged, the police seize the drugs and leave the scene. The sex worker immediately needs to secure drugs and engages in riskier-than-normal behaviour to do so. I reminded the minister to consider the continuing murder of Indigenous women and girls, some of whom had been engaged in the sex trade, and asked her, "How can we not do this?"

Minister Bennett seemed moved by these arguments, and especially by the idea of removing police from what is essentially a health-care issue. She asked me why we did not apply for a higher carry threshold, and I told her that we had altered our initial application to include higher thresholds, but had had to revert to our original limits after police threatened to withdraw their support for the City's application. She confirmed former minister Hajdu's opinion that the prime minister and cabinet would never approve an application over the objections of the police.

The meeting ended with a discussion about the province of British Columbia's parallel decriminalization application. She asked why we did not just work with the province.

I stated that I truly believed that decriminalization was a no-go policy for Premier Horgan, and that the province had submitted its own application only because we had forced them into it. I told her we had called the province's bluff and did not trust them to follow through with their recently submitted decriminalization application. I also emphasized that Health Canada had an obligation to respond to the City of Vancouver's application, as it had been officially received by the ministry, and, as politely as I could, I asked her to imagine how a rejection letter bearing her signature would be received. I threw everything I had at the minister in the hope that I could move her to approve our application. The meeting ended cordially with promises to follow up.

Meanwhile, unbeknownst to me, my friend and former colleague NDP MP Gord Johns made a move on his own. On December 15, 2021, Johns introduced to the House of Commons private member's bill C-216—"An Act to amend the Controlled Drugs and Substances Act and to enact the Expungement of Certain Drug-related Convictions Act and the National Strategy on Substance Use Act (Health-Based Approach to Substance Use Act)." The main point of Bill C-216 was to amend the Controlled Drugs and Substances Act and the Criminal Code to remove the criminalization of possession of small amounts of hard drugs for personal use or simple possession, while leaving in place laws concerning the commercial use or sale of hard drugs, better known as trafficking.[75]

When the private members' lottery draw results were published for the forty-fourth Parliament on December 1,

2021, Gord Johns found himself fourth on the order of precedence. This lucky outcome meant not only that he had the power to trigger a vote in the House of Commons on practically any bill or motion he cared to put forward, but also that a vote on his bill would in all likelihood occur before an election was called. On February 10, 2022, the parliamentary clerk informed the House of Commons that Gord Johns would put forward c-216, and that members of Parliament would for the first time be compelled to vote on whether to decriminalize hard drugs. The importance of Johns's bill would soon become apparent to all decriminalization advocates.

I heard very little from Minister Bennett as she considered whether she would approve Vancouver's application, bc's application, neither application, or both applications. On April 6, Minister Malcolmson told reporters that Minister Bennett was considering granting the provincial request for a federal decriminalization exemption, but only if the cumulative carry threshold was reduced from 4.5 to 2.5 grams[76]—to which Minister Bennett simply replied in the media that no decision had yet been made. Drug policy reform advocates went ballistic at the possibility of reduced thresholds.

A few weeks later, it was reported that c-216 would come before Parliament for a vote on or about June 1. This was problematic for the Trudeau minority government. Bill c-216 was unlikely to pass because the Conservatives would join with Trudeau and many in his Liberal caucus to vote against it. However, the Bill c-216 vote could massively fracture Trudeau's caucus if too many backbenchers split off and voted with the NDP. Liberal Party members had already made decriminalization official party policy in 2018, and several Liberal MPs, including Toronto MP Nathaniel Erskine-Smith, were openly campaigning for C-216. Bennett could no longer stall and needed to decide if and to whom she would grant an exemption. Time was running out.

9

"WE GOT DECRIM!"

A T THE END OF MAY, I WAS CONTACTED BY MINISTER Bennett's office to schedule a May 30 in-person meeting, two days before Gord Johns's Bill C-216 was to hit the floor of the House of Commons for the all-important second-reading vote on June 1. Minister Bennett came to city hall the next day to inform me the federal government would announce it was approving the Province of British Columbia's request for a Controlled Drugs and Substances Act Section 56 exemption and would announce the decision the next day, May 31. I was elated! Not only had we succeeded in decriminalizing drugs in Vancouver, but our effort had forced a province-wide policy change. What a moment!

Minister Bennett asked me to attend the media conference where she would announce that decriminalization was coming to BC. We had succeeded in decriminalizing drugs despite Premier Horgan's obvious opposition to the policy, despite my main ally, Patty Hajdu, losing her portfolio, despite harsh attacks from drug user activists and health researchers, and despite a deeply fractured council who were either on the sidelines about supporting me in the next election or doing all they could to defeat me. As soon as Bennett left, I ran back to the mayor's offices and shouted, "We got decrim!" Neil, Anita, Alvin, Alex and Laurie jumped from their seats and we high-fived all around. The best part was that my deputy chief of staff, Lauren Reid, was away from the office, and I got to call her and say it again: "We got decrim!" This was a win for us and, more importantly, a win for Susan Havelock and her brother Ray and the thousands of people who had died or lost loved ones because of a government-caused public health policy disaster.

The media conference was a surprisingly low-key affair, considering the magnitude of what was being announced: as of January 31, 2023, the possession of small amounts of a large range of illicit drugs would be decriminalized across the province. Dr. Nel Wieman, acting chief medical officer of the First Nations Health Authority, opened the proceedings, followed by Minister Bennett, BC minister of mental health and addictions Sheila Malcolmson, and BC provincial health officer Dr. Bonnie Henry, with me speaking last.

Minister Bennett opened by thanking us all for attending, and then, turning to me, added, "Every day, I think of that meeting with you in the fall as you described your weekly Monday morning reports on the opioid deaths in your city in the previous week. Every day I am reminded of the urgency of this crisis." After announcing her decision to approve BC's decriminalization request, Minister Bennett made it clear that the decision had not been taken lightly, and stressed it was not legalizing hard drugs.

Calling the federal government's approval "a major step in changing how we view addiction and drug use," Minister Malcolmson also offered congratulations and remarks. Dr. Henry said this was a "very, very important next step," that it was "hard to believe we've actually got here," and that when she advised the BC provincial government to decriminalize drugs in 2018, "there was not a lot of support for it at any level." I finished out the speeches by also thanking everyone involved, and as I watched the ministers take questions from the media, I felt I had finally passed off the baton on this issue.[77]

Predictably, long-standing decriminalization advocates offered criticism or lukewarm support, while drug policy reform opponents were damning. Lisa Lapointe, BC's chief coroner, said, "It's been described as decriminalization. I'm not sure that it is."[78] The Canadian Drug Policy Coalition stated, "We support policy that moves the needle forward; however, it is disappointing that decriminalization under the model announced on May 31 will not protect all people who use drugs from the harms of criminalization."[79] Centreright national Conservative Party leader Pierre Poilievre took to Twitter to say, "Decriminalizing deadly drug use is the opposite of compassionate. Those struggling with addiction need treatment & recovery. Drug dealers need strong policing & tough sentences."[80]

The drama around drug decriminalization was not quite over. Gord Johns's Bill C-216 came to the House of Commons for a vote the next day, June 1. However, the Trudeau government's announcement approving decriminalization in BC the previous day had taken the air out of Johns's balloon. While he fought valiantly to get the support he needed from back-bench Liberal MPs, the vote failed with 71 yeas and 248 nays. Johns had managed to secure support from all twenty-five NDP MPs and from fourteen backbench Liberal MPs, but the bill died when 131 Liberals and 117 Conservative MPs voted no. Gord Johns was crushed, but in a subsequent call I said to him that he had played a massive role in getting decriminalization in BC, as his bill had pushed Minister Bennett to accelerate her decision to approve the BC application so her cabinet could vote no to decriminalizing drugs country-wide while avoiding a much larger Liberal backbench revolt.

There was a lot still to do. The province of British Columbia and Health Canada had to work out further exemption details; training modules needed to be designed and added to police education curriculum; the public had to be made aware of how these changes would affect their lives. However, no one needed to fight to ensure all these steps would happen. Canadians would finally be able to see decriminalization in action, starting in early 2023, and judge for themselves if this was a practice they wanted in other parts of the country.

10

WELCOME TO CRUEL VANCOUVER

I WAS NO LONGER MAYOR WHEN ILLICIT DRUGS WERE DECRIM- inalized in British Columbia on January 31, 2023. Between October 2018 and October 2022, I had worked day and night to hold the motley city-council crew together, see the city through COVID-19, approve a record number of affordable homes, accelerate transit construction and decriminalize drugs, among myriad other accomplishments of which I am very proud. Simultaneously, Ken Sim had grown obsessed with winning the mayor's chair after losing the 2018 race by just under a thousand votes, and he used these four years to ready himself for a 2022 rematch. The 2018 Vancouver muni- cipal election had been unremarkable, even boring. But powerful new groups opposed to decriminalization and other progressive policies had since emerged to actively oppose my 2022 re-election bid, with Ken Sim gleefully jumping to the front of the parade, Pied-Pipering his way to victory by playing law-and-order tunes. Get ready for cruel Vancouver.

NIMBYs

I was elected in 2018 with a mandate to build more affordable rental housing across the city and places where those
living with mental health and addiction issues could lay
their heads. Where past councils had focused on building
condominiums in less affluent neighbourhoods, I promoted
building affordable social housing throughout the city,
including wealthy neighbourhoods that had been insulated
from change by past councils for decades. Opposition to my
new program was constant and fierce. Hundreds of wealthy
West Side residents jammed public hearings to defend the
"character" of their neighbourhoods, claiming low-rise rental
buildings, some with vacancy-controlled units for those
making minimum wage, some heavily subsidized for those
living in poverty, would destroy everything they had worked
so hard to build. It was common for mostly white, mega-rich
residents of these neighbourhoods to claim the City was
dropping "ghettos" into their treasured neighbourhoods
when they came to speak at council meetings.[81] I witnessed
hundreds of racist and classist rants from these speakers,
with Indigenous, Black and People of Colour (IBPOC) and
those suffering from mental health and drug use challenges
bearing the brunt of this violence.

One proposed West Side social housing project that
came to council in 2022 faced a group of opponents including medical doctors, university professors, school principals,
Catholic clergy, high-priced lobbyists and hundreds of the
city's most affluent residents, who spent thousands of dollars on a campaign to scare council into not approving a new

thirteen-floor building for local low-income and homeless residents. I remember I had to shut down the first speaker who went on a rant about "junkies" endangering local children. The whole hearing was a shameful display by those who have so much against those who have so little. It was anything but Christian. I managed to convince enough councillors to vote with me and support the project, while councillor Sarah Kirby-Yung, who went on to stand with Ken Sim as an ABC candidate, voted against the project.

The debate around these projects reveals the true face of those who have almost always controlled Vancouver since it was incorporated in 1886. The phenomenon is often referred to with the innocuous term *NIMBY*, for "not in my backyard." But four years of chairing public hearings where people with significant financial means fearlessly punch down on the neediest in society have suggested to me that *NIMBY* does not accurately reflect the overtly racist, classist and discriminatory motivations inherent in their actions. The people who showed up to these meetings, and on whom Ken Sim depended for votes, either had enough money to easily afford homes in the city's most expensive neighbourhoods, or had inherited properties, or had taken out huge mortgages to follow the rule of owning the worst house in the "best" area. They feared any change that would lower their property values, including any government investment that would bring people of lower means into their neighbourhoods, including transit, rental housing, and social and health services.

I did everything I could during my term as mayor to build rental and social housing in affluent neighbourhoods, including working with local First Nations to help their communities develop homes on their stolen lands and increasing transit accessibility by accelerating the Broadway Subway extension to the University of British Columbia. Where many homeowners from the West Side publicly lament Vancouver's inaccessible housing market and high levels of homelessness, they mount sophisticated and well-funded campaigns to stop even the smallest change in their own neighbourhoods. Practically every new project coming before council in this part of the city activated a hornet's nest of angry settlers, some of whom spouted blatant white supremacist rhetoric. I whacked the hive every few weeks to get people off the streets and into homes they could afford, so I was not surprised that NIMBYs voted for Sim in 2022, as he was seen as someone who would stop these intrusions.

Gentrifiers

The motivations of the second group of opponents, which I call "gentrifiers," are like those of NIMBYs. These are middle-class professionals who buy the best home in the "worst" neighbourhood, then work to attract government investment while driving out lower-income residents. Gentrifiers welcome new luxury homes, schools and recreational facilities in their neighbourhoods, but fight against social service investments. Many gentrifiers purchase homes in areas adjacent to the lowest-income neighbourhoods, such as Vancouver's impoverished Downtown Eastside. This location choice often brings frequent and direct interactions between newly arrived upwardly mobile residents and long-term residents experiencing poverty and mental-health and addiction challenges.

Gentrifiers' gamble of buying homes in low-income neighbourhoods initially paid off and they became millionaires when property values skyrocketed. Funky businesses and restaurants followed, as did powerful local lobby groups demanding more police presence and increased municipal services. Then COVID-19 hit. During the pandemic, health officials imposed physical distancing rules to reduce the spread of the virus. As mentioned, physical distancing orders forced SRO housing operators to suspend their overnight-guest policy, driving hundreds of guests from their accommodations and away from their overdose prevention services. They had no choice but to sleep rough in parks and public spaces in neighbourhoods now inhabited by gentrifiers.

Local gentrifiers panicked as their parks began to fill up with local pandemic SRO refugees, and activities like drug use, petty crime and sex work usually hidden behind the doors of the decaying, ancient hotels came into public view. I rejected calls to pursue court injunctions empowering police to clear these parks, and instead made it my mission to secure emergency housing funding from senior governments to open new shelters, convert three-star hotels into long-term accommodations, and erect temporary modular housing. In the end, I secured over $1 billion in housing funding over my four years in office, and the parks eventually emptied as people moved into their new homes. However, while we secured this housing, local gentrifiers joined NIMBYs to kick those needing the most help during the pandemic, while denouncing me for ruining their neighbourhoods.

Gentrifiers also opposed measures to save those dying from poisoned drugs. A good example of this behaviour came when residents near the main downtown hospital— St. Paul's—organized to stop a new overdose prevention site (OPS) named after Thomus Donaghy—an overdose-prevention peer worker reported to have single-handedly saved thousands of lives.[82] Vancouver Coastal Health had identified the area close to St. Paul's as one of high need and proposed erecting the new OPS within a city-owned build-ing, to replace temporary OPS sites situated in tents and vans. Focusing on this former industrial area once known for nightclubs and sex worker strolls, past councils had approved luxury condo towers that were snatched up by many investor suburbanites who had never lived in a densely populated urban space. Local groups organized to stop city council from approving a lease for the new OPS, which passed despite opposition from councillors Sarah Kirby-Yung and Lisa Dominato, who ran with Sim in 2018 and again in 2022. Speakers from these groups used hateful and discriminatory language throughout the hearings, and I had to caution or cut many of them off as meeting chair.

Haters

Ken Sim's election parade was also joined by what I deem "haters." These polarizing groups sought to stoke fear and div-ision among residents during the pandemic and the recovery period. They included COVID-19 anti-vaxxers, the Pacific Prosperity Network, and the Vancouver Police Union.[83]

The anti-vaxxer movement emerged almost as soon as governments began to implement COVID-19 mitigation strategies, such as shutting down businesses or limiting their activities and requiring physical distancing in public places. Unlike other major cities, Vancouver was fortunate to avoid total lockdowns because of our mild climate and high vaccination rates. Despite this, a growing group of anti-vaxxers continually defied public health orders, keeping their businesses and restaurants open to inside visitors, resulting in fines from the City and health authorities.[84] This national movement peaked when a so-called "freedom convoy" used large trucks to shut down the city of Ottawa and other parts of the country. Anti-vaxxers planned similar blockading activities for Vancouver, targeting local hospitals and health-care workers.

We managed to stop trucker convoys from blocking the downtown during the February 2022 turmoil, when I told protesters, "Vancouver doesn't want you here. Make your point and then go home," which prompted massive social media attacks on me from around the globe, including from US senator Ted Cruz.[85] These attacks by this powerful far-right movement and its bots increased during the pandemic and election, and continue today. Federal Conservative Party leader and Ottawa freedom-convoy sympathizer Pierre Poilievre got into the act with his own attack video which caught the eyes of over 150,000 YouTube viewers, and he piled on with negative House of Commons speeches against me in the pre–municipal election period.

The Pacific Prosperity Network was also on Ken Sim's attack team. PPN follows the same "pro-freedom" and "pro-free enterprise" cry as the anti-vaxxers, and takes advantage of loopholes in election rules by generating and promoting attack campaigns not subject to election spending limits.[86] The core of their contribution to Sim's campaign was a PPN-sponsored video entitled *Vancouver Is Dying*. With nearly three million views, this hour-long video is a slick, fear-based attack ad against me, my support for health-based solutions to the mental health and addictions crisis, and those suffering from trauma. PPN also posted online petitions, including one entitled "No More Free Drugs." I had no way to counter this massive, unregulated smear campaign, which, sadly, local media helped promote on a regular basis.

Another group taking advantage of a pandemic-beset population was the Vancouver Police Union. While I remain on good terms with Vancouver police chief constable Adam Palmer and still believe he was key to decriminalizing drugs, the same cannot be said for some of his executive members and the VPU president. The VPU went ballistic after I held a media conference in June 2020, declaring the Vancouver Police Department to be systemically racist, and calling for, and securing, a provincial inquiry to initiate police reform.[87] I made these comments in response to a report on street checks showing clear police bias against IBPOC residents, as well as the arrest and handcuffing of Torianne Tweedie and Maxwell Johnson, and other incidents for which police would not apologize or admit wrongdoing.[88] The Vancouver Police Union responded to my calls for truth and reform by launching an attack website and petitions against me, and, for the first time in the organization's history, the VPU outright endorsed a mayoral candidate, after Ken Sim promised to massively increase the police budget.

The ties between PPN, the VPU and Sim associates emerged at an event just before the municipal vote, during a PPN-hosted screening and panel discussion of *Vancouver Is Dying*. The event featured a panel with executive producer Angelo Isidorou, director Aaron Gunn and VPU president Ralph Kaisers. Isidorou was a board member of the Non-Partisan Association (Ken Sim's party in 2018) who, along with seven of his colleagues, launched a vicious, and ultimately unsuccessful, defamation lawsuit against me for calling the NPA board out for failing "to stop hate spreading within their party," after media reported some NPA executive members having links to far-right groups.[89] Gunn has been described in the media as a "far-right extremist" and rejected as a candidate for leader of the provincial (centre-right) BC Liberal Party, after party brass concluded "Gunn's candidacy would be inconsistent with the B.C. Liberal party's commitment to reconciliation, diversity and acceptance of all British Columbians."[90]

Pulling all these threads together, many of Ken Sim's supporters in the 2022 election rallied around a long-held Vancouver value—colonialism. West Side NIMBYs with homes on stolen land wanted to keep their neighbourhoods free of those they feel are of lesser intrinsic value—including those from whom they had stolen the land in the first place. Gentrifiers colonized low-income areas and then, after some nice words, worked hard to displace those with mental health and addiction issues who had been there first.

Anti-vaxxers who were often associated with hate groups used the pandemic to spread division and target minorities and the most vulnerable. The ultra-wealthy backers of PPN sought to become even wealthier by spreading propaganda to convince Vancouver residents their vulnerable neighbours somehow required punishment as opposed to care. Finally, the Vancouver Police Union shamefully repeated past Canadian police actions and protected and promoted the interests of colonizers, while taking advantage of the pandemic trauma to increase their already outrageously generous budget.

In 2021, Sim had broken from his old party, the NPA, to launch A Better City (ABC). ABC's 2022 campaign was policy-lite but very well-funded and organized. Its over $2 million campaign had a classic law and order theme centred on a promise to hire a hundred new police officers and nurses to address homelessness and street disturbances caused by residents suffering from mental health and addiction difficulties. Sim's campaign manager, Kareem Allam, later admitted the pledge to hire new police was just a gimmick to win votes: "One hundred new police officers, we already have 1,600, so adding another 100, so what's that, 4 or 5 percent new police? Is that really going to have a dramatic impact on reducing crime? Probably not."[91] Sim also parroted the everything-is-broken theme raised by NIMBYs, gentrifiers, anti-vaxxers, the Pacific Prosperity Network and the Vancouver Police Union.

For my own campaign, I was proud to put together a slate of great people who would stand with me in 2022 under a new "Forward Together" banner, including my wife, Jeanette Ashe. We spent $1 million campaigning on a platform of continuing the policies I had worked on over the last four years, including proposing the approval of hundreds of thousands of new affordable homes and the implementation of safer-supply measures to reduce illicit drug-related deaths. It was all for naught, and on October 15, my Forward Together team was crushed. Of the 36 percent of eligible voters casting ballots, 50 percent voted for Sim, while 30 percent voted for me—the same vote percentage I had received in 2018. All ABC candidates were elected to office and my entire slate was wiped out. Sim and his allies' campaign of scaring Vancouverites into voting for an old-style, colonial approach to running Vancouver had worked perfectly, and Sim and his ABC majority council were authorized to punish vulnerable people in what now is beginning to feel like cruel Vancouver.

Sim City

Although only seven months into their four-year term at the time of writing, Sim has already started to deliver for his supporters. City council quickly moved on Sim's top priority of funding a hundred new police officers, increasing the police budget by nearly 12 percent. Despite promising during the election that he could deliver new police officers without service cuts or property tax increases, Sim voted to increase property taxes by 10.7 percent to pay for increased policing costs, the largest hike in a generation.[92]

Shortly after the police budget was approved in March 2023, police moved to clear dozens of Downtown Eastside residents sheltering on sidewalks and in alleys.

In the epicentre of the illicit drug–related death crisis and home of critical overdose-prevention services, over a hundred police officers blocked portions of the DTES for days so sanitation engineers could toss tents and other possessions into garbage trucks. Police barred media and cut off local traffic-camera feeds in the area during portions of the operation. The decampment occurred despite Sim not having secured sufficient shelter spaces for those being forcibly evicted from their makeshift homes, meaning people would now sleep without any cover during some of the worst weather of the year.

The police-led DTES decampment operation was condemned by many, including Federal Housing Advocate Marie-Josée Houle. Houle called on Mayor Sim "to put a moratorium in place on dismantling encampments," as "forced evictions of encampments are a violation of human rights" and "increase risks to people's health and safety due to isolation, exposure, fire, overdose, and violence."[93] The British Columbia Federation of Labour issued a statement calling for an immediate halt to the operation and condemning "the callous, dehumanizing tactics used by Mayor Ken Sim's administration in forcibly dismantling encampments in Vancouver's Downtown Eastside...The greatest impact will be felt by Indigenous and racialized people, those facing accessibility barriers, trans and gender-diverse people, and others over-represented in poverty and homelessness."[94]

In addition to embracing a new police-led approach to addressing Vancouver's mental health and addictions crisis, Sim cut a $7,500 arts grant for drug users in the DTES to create memorials to those who have died from toxic drug overdoses.[95] This punitive action spurred a local backlash, to which Sim responded by voting for a motion by which city staff must now monitor the public comments of grant recipients and defund those critical of mayor and council.[96] Finally, Sim seems poised to roll back proven harm reduction measures like overdose prevention sites. ABC councillor Peter Meiszner stated in April that the Thomus Donaghy overdose prevention site in a leased city building near St. Paul's Hospital will be shut because of "concern from residents about things like discarded needles on the sidewalk, some of the structures that have been set up and also just some of the interactions with people who have been congregating."[97]

Life-saving harm reduction measures such as needle exchanges, supervised consumption sites, safer-supply programs and now decriminalization were only secured through an immense effort against all odds. But now that NIMBYs and gentrifiers have banded together with far-right anti-vaxxers and the police union to elect Sim and his majority, illicit drug–related deaths are likely to be a merely inconvenient, but largely avoided, truth for the current council. There is little hope Sim will champion new proactive measures to reduce the ever-increasing number of drug-related deaths in Vancouver or provide other services, such as social or affordable housing, as it will scare away his base. There is a very strong chance he will continue to more fully embrace criminalization and cruelty toward those needing the most help. I hope he proves me wrong.

11

SAVING SUSAN HAVELOCK

I OFTEN IMAGINE SUSAN HAVELOCK'S LAST MINUTES OF LIFE. Slowly nodding off under that awning in the early hours of the morning, avoiding the rain. Overdosing alone after taking an unknown mixture of drugs she needed to survive, purchased from organized criminals with whatever money she had. In and out of rehab for decades, but still ending up here after all these years, still fearing arrest or police seizing her drugs. We should have done more for Susan. We need to do better for everyone else.

It is hard to admit, but I believe Susan would have died from toxic drugs even if she had survived the few remaining months before her behaviour were decriminalized under the Health Canada exemption. Before decriminalization, if police stopped her for, say, loitering, and she was found to possess a small quantity of hard drugs, there was a miniscule chance they would have arrested or detained her in the municipal jail. However, they certainly would have seized her drugs, forcing Susan to desperately and immediately get more from elsewhere, undertaking risky activities to secure funds and buy drugs from an unfamiliar source, increasing her risk of harmful or violent encounters and using drugs with even higher levels of toxicity.

With decriminalization, if police had stopped Susan for loitering and she had been found to possess a small quantity of the drugs listed in the provincial application, she would not have been charged with possession, nor would her drugs have been seized if she was carrying less than 2.5 grams. Not arresting Susan or seizing her drugs might have slightly reduced Susan's level of risk over the short term, but it would likely have done very little to reduce her long-term risks. She still would have been stigmatized and treated as an outsider in her city. She still would have been impoverished and underhoused. Treatment still would have been very hard to secure, and the current programs would have offered only a temporary break until she relapsed. The trauma against which she struggled would still have been present. Under the current conditions, Susan most likely would have ended up under the same awning, or another one like it, slipping off into sleep, forever.

This vision is even more horrifying when you consider that thousands of Vancouverites use drugs, as do hundreds of thousands of people living in Canada. Our national approach to criminalizing drug users, coupled with the toxic drug supply rapidly spreading from west to east, suggests there is little hope the carnage will end until, perhaps, there is no one left. It is even more vexing considering how difficult it was to secure what in the end will be the relatively inconsequential policy change of decriminalizing drugs in British Columbia.

No one in power really wanted to decriminalize drugs in British Columbia. Not Prime Minister Trudeau. Not Premier John Horgan. Not me—at least, not until federal health minister Patty Hajdu called me to offer a plausible way forward and, together, we made it politically impossible for the British Columbia provincial government to maintain its status quo position, and, subsequently, politically impossible for Hajdu's successor, federal minister of mental health and addictions Dr. Carolyn Bennett, not to sign either Vancouver's or British Columbia's decriminalization exemption application. It took all these machinations to secure a policy change that would probably not have saved Susan's life. That it is so hard to secure even minor drug policy reforms leaves me wondering what comes next and what we might practically do to lengthen and improve the lives of those living with substance use disorder.

Susan's World

Good policies, including those concerning illicit drug use, require policy-makers to clearly identify the problem they wish to address and understand the surrounding context. The policy problem here is simple: too many illicit drug–related deaths. The context, however, is complicated and ever-evolving.

None of us will truly know why Susan started using drugs, but her brother Ray told me she started using cocaine after visiting a Hollywood film set in her hometown of Hope, British Columbia, in the early 1980s. The seventeen-year-old Susan feared needles, so she would not inject drugs like heroin, but snorting or smoking cocaine seemed okay—just as it does to the nearly 9 percent of Canadians reporting they have tried cocaine at least once in their lives.[98] When Susan started using, regular cocaine consumers would usually overdose only when the concentration of the drug was unexpectedly intense. It was expensive to be a drug user in these early years, as organic drugs are produced by growing and refining opium and coca leaves in foreign places, creating expensive processed drugs that traffickers import to dealers, who then sell them to users at a huge markup. I always, and probably naïvely, think of Al Pacino's film *Scarface* when I imagine the 1980s drug market.

The drug market in which Susan secured her cocaine changed over the years, most radically when organized criminals discovered they could dramatically reduce costs by cutting all traditional organic drugs with fentanyl or other synthetic opioids, first produced in foreign labs, but later, increasingly, in domestic ones. Experienced and novice users began to overdose when they thought they were taking organic drugs but were actually injecting, snorting or smok-·ing a mixed substance up to a hundred times more powerful than their regular dosage. The intensity of the new substances also served to increase user tolerance to a point where the effect of traditional organic drugs was seldom sufficient, and users began to simply seek fentanyl or other synthetic opioids to satisfy the demands of their disorder.

Whereas Susan and others with substance use disorders are extremely sensitive to changes in the local drug market, governments are very slow to react—especially when drug use is such a taboo subject. In the age of fentanyl, the government offers drug users like Susan four options to manage their disorder. Susan eventually died of the first option, which is the current default for Canadians using illicit drugs:

1. **Torturous death:** Continued, unsupervised exposure to unregulated toxic drugs, with a high likelihood of multiple overdoses, permanent brain injury and, eventually, death.
2. **Ineffective treatment:** Voluntary, abstinence-focused treatment programs with a low probability of long-term success.
3. **Incarceration:** Forced abstinence with sporadic access to poisoned drugs in jail or prison.
4. **Ineffective safer supply:** Limited and often overly restrictive drug substitution programs.

Susan had tried the second option, *ineffective treatment*, many times, according to her brother Ray. Those suffering from alcohol use disorder are commonly offered programs where abstinence is the end goal for voluntary participants, with those tempted to deviate from the path offered support and coaching. The implied or overt goal of these programs is to learn to forever deny cravings, re-enter the workforce, and live an alcohol-free life. There are few legal consequences for those breaking from alcohol abstinence, as they are usually allowed to re-enter rehabilitation programs, and alcohol is a regulated addictive substance for which there are, for the most part, no penalties for legal production, distribution or possession. Abstinence-focused programs are effective for many, especially if participants subscribe to other values of the usually Christian-oriented program providers. However, they can prove inaccessible or ineffective for those who do not already believe or come to adopt these associated belief systems.

Similar abstinence-focused programs are usually offered to those with non-alcohol-based substance use disorders, like Susan. Such programs can work for a small number of participants, but up to 90 percent relapse. Unlike those with alcohol-based substance use disorders, those with non-alcohol-based substance use disorders immediately re-enter the criminal world upon relapse, seeking banned, unregulated substances with which they play Russian roulette with every dose. In addition, even short periods of abstinence leave users with reduced tolerance, making them even more vulnerable to the toxic drugs they secure upon exiting a treatment program.

Susan voluntarily entered many Christian- and non-Christian-centred drug treatment programs. To help her on her journey, she was provided with poverty-level social service support, and a permanent police presence empowered to harass her, arrest her or seize her drugs if she stumbled along the way. Susan relapsed shortly after exiting these programs, like most other program participants. This option set Susan up for failure by offering her treatment options not based on science or her needs, but on our collective denial-based fantasy. Of course, Susan defaulted back to Option 1, *torturous death*, after exiting Option 2.

Susan also tried Option 3, *incarceration*, at least nine times. According to Ray, this was her preferred option of the four available, as she had a place to sleep every night and regular meals. There was occasional access to Christian-based abstinence programs that did not work for her no matter how hard she tried, as well as an intermittent, smuggled supply of drugs with incredibly unpredictable potency, from which she was at a much higher risk of overdosing. Susan's involuntary participation in Option 3 ended when the court decided she was eligible to return once again to the default, Option 1: *torturous death*.

The fourth and final option for Susan, *ineffective safer supply*, involved Susan being prescribed one of a limited number of legal drugs to replace the illicit drugs on which she had come to depend. Ray described how Susan would contact him, excited about such safer-supply treatment, only to relapse as the prescribed drug failed as an adequate substitute. In addition, these treatment regimes required constant interactions with physicians, who prescribed and monitored Susan's progress, and pharmacists, who often required the patient to go to the pharmacy daily and consume the drug under observation. These high-barrier safer-supply treatment programs failed Susan, as she found it very difficult to jump through all the bureaucratic hoops required for her to participate, only to be prescribed a drug that did not satisfy her body's needs. Susan fell back to Option 1, *torturous death*, when these poorly designed treatment programs inevitably failed.

It is incredibly sad that tens of thousands of Canadian families face these same four options, with the default and most likely outcome being that a drug user they love will experience the worst imaginable end to life. For Canada to retain its reputation as one of the most caring and compassionate countries in which to live, we must do better. Doing better starts with recognizing that the status quo is not working and listening to what peers and the best scientific minds have to say, and then moving beyond our own fears to do what is necessary to end illicit drug-related deaths.

Decriminalizing Drugs in Canada

The most obvious place to start in improving the lives of drug users is to decriminalize drugs across the country. Police play no useful role in improving the lives of drug users, a fact that police leaders themselves recognize, and that has convinced the top Canadian policing organization to advocate for drug decriminalization. Although police may not agree with health-care providers and drug users about drug-carry thresholds, all three groups agree that criminalizing drug users is costly, ineffective and deadly. Vancouver police years ago gave up on arresting drug users for simple possession, indicating the extent to which they feel the laws are out of step with reality and the extraordinary measures they are prepared to take to do what is right—including ignoring their sworn duty to uphold Canadian laws.

However, while Vancouver police seldom arrest those possessing small quantities of illicit drugs, they continue to seize these small amounts from users they encounter. These seemingly unnecessary seizures show that police are nervous about their decision to informally decriminalize drug use. The Vancouver police practice of not arresting those clearly violating Canadian drug laws potentially leaves offi-cers in a difficult position. It is unclear what moral and legal responsibilities an officer has if, say, they do not arrest some-one for possessing small quantities of drugs and do not seize these drugs, and then that person goes on to die from toxic drugs. The safest course for the officer, then, is to seize the drugs and let the person go. This is common practice for other substances, as when police pour out beers belonging to people caught drinking on a beach. But, unlike alcohol drinkers, drug users face very high risks if they are forced to secure illicit drugs in a toxic drug market on short notice and from unknown suppliers.

The burden of deciding whether or not to enforce laws should not fall to the police, and it is irresponsible for federal and provincial legislators to offload such decisions regarding arresting people for drug possession to individual police offi-cers and departments. In simple terms, governments make laws and police enforce laws. Elected decision-makers have failed to perform their duties when police view an issue as so serious and intractable that they stray into the domain of elected policy-makers. That federal and British Columbian political leaders have finally caught up to police in this prov-ince is a welcome sign. However, that drug users are still criminalized in all other provinces and territories puts police in a very difficult position in other Canadian jurisdictions due to the failure of policy-makers to address the overdose crisis spreading across the country.

That Health Canada was willing to accept and strongly consider the City of Vancouver's application for a Section 56 exemption to the Controlled Drugs and Substances Act provides an important example to the rest of the country: it strongly suggests that the federal government would consider similar applications to decriminalize drugs from other municipalities and local health authorities. In this vein, the City of Toronto, through Toronto Public Health, has followed the City of Vancouver's lead and applied for a Section 56 exemption to decriminalize drugs in Canada's largest municipality. Signed by the medical health officer, police chief and city manager, Toronto's application requests an even more permissive exemption than that granted to British Columbia, including all drugs for personal use (where the BC exemption has a set list), and shielding young people from criminalization (where the BC exemption applies only to adults). Also, unlike the Vancouver and BC applications, Toronto's request does not propose a specific carry threshold for what constitutes personal use.[99] Pressure is also mounting in other cities, such as Montreal, to consider similar applications.

The general policy of criminalizing drug users has been roundly rejected by medical health professionals and top law enforcement officials, costs a lot of money, and forces drug users further into deadly shadows. As such, we should just decriminalize the simple possession of small quantities of all drugs in Canada. Perhaps the best way forward is for Canada's thousands of municipal governments to replicate one of the applications on file from Vancouver, Toronto or British Columbia and officially apply to Health Canada to decriminalize drugs within their jurisdiction, making it less politically risky for the federal health minister and her cabinet colleagues to move ahead. If enough municipalities apply, all federal parties will need to realize that Canadians have rejected this policy approach, and will then drop their resistance to nationwide decriminalization. Decriminalization is already the official policy of the federal Liberal and New Democratic parties and has the support of law enforcement and public health officials. This mass application process could be coordinated by the very able Federation of Canadian Municipalities—the national voice of municipal governments representing twenty-one hundred municipalities, in which more than 92 percent of all Canadians reside.

Toward Effective Treatment Options

Conservative leader Pierre Poilievre and other right-leaning politicians are correct in insisting that governments invest too little in drug treatment services. My understanding from talking with drug users is that it is very difficult to hang on and wait weeks or months to be admitted to an often very expensive treatment program once you decide to seek help. But I disagree with centre-right politicians who insist that abstinence-based treatment should be the sole option on offer.

Instead, we now require a range of treatment programs based on the physical, psychological, psychiatric and cultural requirements of those in need. Treatment must meet users where they live to have any chance of succeeding. Offering only Christianity-based, unicultural, abstinence-style programs is, for example, unlikely to help those traumatized by the Canadian Indigenous Genocide, as it is often difficult for those who suffered in church- or state-run residential schools, in the Sixties Scoop, or from related intergenerational trauma to embrace such a colonial approach to well-being.

The best peer-reviewed scientific research indicates that Canada needs to expand safer-supply programs for those with substance use disorders. Again, the premise of these programs is to help participants reduce, but not eliminate, their drug consumption, abandoning the idea that they will ever abstain—at least, not until they have come to terms with the underlying trauma driving their drug use. It is counterproductive and dangerous to have someone complete abstinence-based treatment, only to have them relapse and go back to the street to secure the drugs on which they depend, then go back into treatment, and so on. What Susan needed was a safer-supply treatment option to help her live a better life through maintaining, as safely as possible, what was most likely a life of sustained drug use.

Available in Canada on a limited basis, safer-supply programs substitute prescribed alternatives to the toxic illegal drug supply to people who are at high risk of overdosing. The most widely available of these safer-supply programs is traditional opioid agonist therapy (OAT), where, since the 1960s, doctors have prescribed long-acting opioids, such as methadone, and, more recently, hydromorphone and suboxone, to stabilize the cycle of being high and withdrawing. Invented in Vancouver in 1959, methadone maintenance programs still prove effective for some, with as many as 100,000 Canadians currently enrolled.[100]

But OAT began to fail to work for many with substance use disorders when fentanyl and other synthetic opioids began to dominate the drug supply. As a result, concerned practitioners like Vancouver-based Dr. Christy Sutherland have trialled successful programs where patients are pre-scribed diacetylmorphine—the medical term for heroin—or slow-release fentanyl patches.[101] Some patients in these types of programs pay for their prescriptions; for others, the drugs are free. The policing experts I have spoken to about this would prefer these substitute drugs to be free, as it would reduce petty crime connected with this issue. However, these programs currently serve only a handful of patients, with involved doctors like Sutherland risking their licences to serve their patients.

There are thousands of Canadian drug users who would benefit from safer-supply treatment programs using a wider array of more effective drugs. While a limited number of small-sample scientific trials indicate that such programs effectively stabilize the daily routines and health of drug users, the method by which they are currently delivered is not scalable. Imagine the bottlenecks that would be created in doctors' offices, clinics and hospitals if, for example, the 400,000 Canadians with type 1 diabetes were required to visit a pharmacy once or even two, three, four or five times a day to secure the insulin they need, inject the drug under the observation of the pharmacy team, and renew their prescrip-tion every month. This is essentially what happens in these safer-supply programs and why these high-barrier programs often fail those who enroll.

While some argue we should re-legalize heroin, cocaine and other hard drugs, as we did with cannabis, I am not sure this is the best way forward. Cannabis is widely used through-out the population. In one 2015 scientific survey completed before cannabis was re-legalized, almost half the Canadian population over the age of fifteen indicated they had used cannabis at least once in their lifetime.[102] Its criminalization merely saddled law enforcement officials and users with unnecessary burdens and provided an unjustified revenue stream for organized crime. However, only 18 percent of Canadians report having used controlled and illicit drugs like heroin and cocaine during their lifetime, suggesting it would be a mistake to allow private-sector operators to produce and sell these drugs in locally licensed shops, a situation that would likely increase consumption by non-users in the general population. But it would also appear that strict prohibition is causing unjustifiable and significant harm to our families, friends and neighbours.

One way forward, for which I officially advocated when I was mayor, is through what are called "compassion clubs," where non-profit societies are permitted to hand out clean, tested drugs to those enrolled in their programs. Club members are not required to jump through the hoops associated with safer-supply studies. Instead, drugs come from the current, illegal market or, preferably, from firms such as Fair Price Pharma, which is licensed by the government to legally produce heroin and other drugs.[103] The compassion-club model is based on those used before cannabis legalization to distribute cannabis to people suffering from cancer and chronic-pain conditions. Decriminalization and safer-supply treatment through compassion clubs have a real chance of reducing illicit drug–related deaths, while improving the lives of all Canadians. In combination, these two measures would reduce the risk for those struggling with substance use disorders, while striking a major blow to organized crime and reducing crime rates.

I imagine how these services would have worked for Susan. Instead of breaking the law to secure the money needed to buy drugs from organized criminals, then using untested and toxic drugs alone, Susan could have joined a peer-operated compassion club where she could have safely secured the drugs she needed from a regulated pharmaceutical company, without fear of poisonous substances, arrest or police seizing her drugs. Once stabilized, she could have sought counselling and therapy to help her deal with her trauma. However, there is no doubt her success would also depend on securing safe housing and enough money to provide for her daily needs. The police, medical community and peers, as well as families who have lost loved ones, all know this is the only way forward. It just needs political will to succeed.

I think about all those public hearings when angry, wealthy people travel in their expensive cars from their beautiful homes to city hall to oppose a small rental building because it would bring "junkies" to their neighbourhood. I think about Conservative leader Pierre Poilievre referring to the very neighbourhood in which Susan died as "hell on earth," not because he cares about people like Susan but because he wants to secure votes from anti-vaxxer bigots, or to scare moderate voters into siding with anti-vaxxer bigots. I think of the social media influencers and their wealthy backers seeking to attract followers by posting videos of the most vulnerable people in our country, who have hit the lowest point in their lives and are in absolute pain and misery. I think about the Vancouver Police Union, which, instead of standing up for those needing the most help, exploited them to pad its budgets. It is so shameful.

I understand that the level of illicit drug–related death is hard to comprehend. It is for me too. It helps for me to think of the thousands of people who have died in the city over which I presided for four years, and to picture them filling every chair in Vancouver's historic twenty-eight-hundred-seat Orpheum Theatre. I picture myself onstage, trying to explain why I did not do more to help, but I can never seem to find the right words. I think we all need to picture ourselves on similar stages in our own communities, and think about what we would say.

ENDNOTES

1   See Appendix.

2   National Institute of Mental Health, "Substance Use and Co-Occurring Mental Disorders."

3   John W. Kingdon, *Agendas, Alternatives, and Public Policies*, 2nd ed. (Pearson, 2010). For an excellent summary and discussion on Kingdon, see Scott Greer, "John W. Kingdon, Agendas, Alternatives, and Public Policies," in *The Oxford Handbook of Classics in Public Policy and Administration*, ed. Martin Lodge, Edward C. Page and Steven J. Balla (Oxford, UK: Oxford University Press, 2015).

4   City of Vancouver, Social Policy and Projects, *Social Indicators and Trends: City of Vancouver Profile 2020* (City of Vancouver, 2020).

5   New Democratic Party, "NDP Motion to Recognize Residential Schools Act as Genocide Gets All-Party Support" (news release, October 27, 2022).

6   The current homeless count "point-in-time" methodology is flawed and dramatically undercounts rough sleepers in Vancouver. See Homelessness Services Association of BC, BC Non-Profit Housing Association, and Urban Matters, *2019 Vancouver Homeless Count* (City of Vancouver, 2019).

7   Mark Gollom, "Bruce McArthur, Robert Pickton and the Toronto 'Missing Men': Links and differences in the Cases," CBC News, February 3, 2018.

8   City of Vancouver, *Social Indicators*.

9   British Columbia Centre for Disease Control, "Top 15 Causes of Death (Ranking) in BC for 2022," bccdc. shinyapps.io/Mortality_Context_ShinyApp.

10   Angus Reid Institute, "Canada's Other Epidemic: As Overdose Deaths Escalate, Majority Favour Decriminalization of Drugs," February 24, 2021, angusreid.org/opioid-crisis-covid.

11   Federal, Provincial, and Territorial Special Advisory Committee on the Epidemic of Opioid Overdoses, "Opioid- and Stimulant-Related Harms in Canada" (Ottawa: Public Health Agency of Canada, March 2023).

12   Angus Reid, "Canada's Other Epidemic."

13 Health Canada, "Detailed Tables: Canadian Alcohol
    and Drugs Survey (CADS) 2019," December 20, 2021,
    www.canada.ca/en/health-canada/services/canadian-
    alcohol-drugs-survey/2019-summary/detailed-tables.
    html.

14 Office of the Chief Coroner, *Report of the Task Force into
    Illicit Narcotic Overdose Deaths in British Columbia*
    (Ministry of Attorney General, 1994), drugpolicy.ca/
    wp-content/uploads/2016/11/Cain-Report.pdf.

15 Travis Lupick, *Fighting for Space: How a Group of Drug
    Users Transformed One City's Struggle with Addiction*
    (Vancouver: Arsenal Pulp Press, 2017), 85.

16 Donald MacPherson, *A Framework for Action: A Four-
    Pillar Approach to Drug Problems in Vancouver* (City of
    Vancouver, 2001).

17 Sean Fine, "Five Fundamental Ways Harper Has
    Changed the Justice System," *Globe and Mail*, May 6,
    2014.

18 Adrienne Smith, "Harper Government Moves to Ban
    Supervised Injection Services for Drug Users in Canada,"
    Pivot, March 23, 2015.

19 "Trudeau Promises to Legalize Marijuana, Not Sell It in
    Depanneurs," *CTV News*, September 3, 2015.

20 Michael Bolen, "NDP's Mulcair Supports
    Decriminalizing Marijuana Possession," *CBC News*,
    August 21, 2015. Jack Layton was a keen proponent of
    legalizing cannabis and made his views known way
    back when he campaigned for leader in 2002.

21 Joan Bryden, "Federal Liberals Endorse Marijuana
    Legalization," *CTV News Vancouver*, January 16, 2012.

22 Mitchel Raphael, "On the Obama Cookie and Trudeau's
    Thoughts on Pot," *Maclean's*, November 16, 2012.

23 "Tom Mulcair Says NDP's Balanced Budget
    Commitment Was His Idea," *CBC News*, October 11, 2015.

24 Kennedy Stewart, "How I Survived Trudeau's Red Tide,"
    The Tyee, November 14, 2015.

25 Graham Slaughter and Michael Shulman, "Mulcair
    Loses Leadership Vote at NDP Convention," *CTV News*,
    April 10, 2016.

26 Kenneth Chan, "NDP Leader Jagmeet Singh Calls for
    Decriminalization of All Drugs for Personal Use," *Daily
    Hive News*, September 23, 2021.

27 Andrew Russell, "Trudeau Says Canada Not Looking
    to Decriminalize Harder Drugs, Experts Call That
    'Irresponsible,'" *Global News*, August 2, 2017.

28 Special Senate Committee on Illegal Drugs, *Cannabis: Our Position for a Canadian Public Policy* (Senate of Canada, September 2002).

29 Laura Stone and Daniel LeBlanc, "Scheer Admits to Smoking Marijuana in the Past, Says He Still Opposes Government's Plan for Legalization," *Globe and Mail*, May 7, 2018.

30 Janice Dickson, "Scheer, Blaney Fundraise off Claim Trudeau Wants to Legalize Heroin," *iPolitics*, January 30, 2017.

31 Andrea Woo, "Federal NDP, Liberals Considering Decriminalization of All Drugs," *Globe and Mail*, February 26, 2018.

32 Woo, "Federal NDP, Liberals Considering Decriminalization."

33 Kathleen Harris, "Ottawa Will Listen, but Won't Act on Party Push to Decriminalize All Drugs: Wilson-Raybould," *CBC News*, April 20, 2018.

34 Mario Canseco, "Carr Extends Lead as Preferred Mayoral Contender in Vancouver," *Research Co.*, May 3, 2018.

35 Canseco, "Stewart, Sim and Campbell Battle in Vancouver Race," *Research Co.*, June 14, 2018.

36 My resignation prompted a by-election in a winnable NDP seat, which Jagmeet Singh won on February 25, 2019, following in the footsteps of former NDP leader Tommy Douglas, who gained his first seat in the House of Commons by winning a by-election in the riding of Burnaby–Coquitlam on October 22, 1962.

37 "A Healthy City: Taking Action on Opioids and Supporting the Downtown Eastside," *Kennedy for Vancouver Mayor 2018*, web.archive.org/web/20181016223843/https://www.kennedystewart.ca/dtes.

38 Terry Schintz and Emily Lazatin, "Kennedy Stewart Set to Launch DTES Task Force to Tackle Opioid Crisis If Elected Mayor," *Global News*, September 20, 2018.

39 Andrea Woo, "Vancouver Mayoral Candidates Weigh In on Drug Decriminalization," *Globe and Mail*, October 19, 2018.

40 City of Vancouver, *Independent Election Task Force: A Review of Campaign Financing by Third Parties and Independent Candidates in Municipal Elections* (June 2019).

41 This incredible assembly of people and organizations included Sarah Blyth from the Overdose Prevention Society, DTES advocate Karen Ward, Chief Medical Health Officer Dr. Patricia Daly, executive medical

director of the BC Centre for Disease Control Dr. Mark Tyndall, former MP Libby Davies, members of local First Nations, the City's People with Lived Experience Advisory Panel, and the Vancouver Community Action Team (CAT). CAT is an extremely valuable resource funded by the Province; co-chaired in 2018 by Mary Clare Zak from the City of Vancouver and Chris Van Veen from Vancouver Coastal Health, it included representatives from the Atira Women's Resource Society, the BC Association for People on Methadone, BC Emergency Health Services, Culture Saves Lives, the First Nations Health Authority, Lookout, the Ministry of Children and Family Development, the Ministry of Social Development and Poverty Reduction, the Metro Vancouver Aboriginal Executive Council, Moms Stop the Harm, Overdose Prevention Sites/PHS Community Services, the Portland Hotel Society, Providence Crosstown Clinic, RainCity Housing, Street Saviours Outreach, Transit Police, the University of British Columbia, Vancouver Coastal Health, the Vancouver Area Network of Drug Users, Vancouver Fire and Rescue Services, the Vancouver Police Department, and the Western Aboriginal Harm Reduction Society. ("Administrative Report," City of Vancouver, December 14, 2018, council.vancouver.ca/20181220/documents/spec1.pdf.)

42 Travis Lupick, "Mayor's Overdose Emergency Task Force Calls for Harm Reduction beyond the Downtown Eastside," *Georgia Straight*, December 18, 2018.

43 Government of British Columbia, "Provincial Health Officer's Report Calls for Decriminalization of People Who Use Drugs," *BC Gov News*, April 24, 2019.

44 Dr. Bonnie Henry, *Stopping the Harm: Decriminalization of People Who Use Drugs in BC— Provincial Health Officer's Special Report* (Office of the Provincial Health Officer, 2019).

45 Michelle Ghoussoub and Rhianna Schmunk, "Top Health Officer Calls on B.C. to 'Urgently' Decriminalize Possession of Illicit Drugs," *CBC News*, April 24, 2019.

46 Kathleen Harris, "Scheer Suggests Liberals Could Decriminalize Hard Drugs, Despite Trudeau's Denial," *CBC News*, October 17, 2019.

47 Simon Little, "Justin Trudeau in Vancouver to Talk Housing, Overdoses, Transit," *Global News*, August 30, 2019.

48 Rachel Browne, "Trudeau Confirms That the Liberals Are Not Looking to Decriminalize Drugs," *Global News*, September 24, 2019.

49 Gary Rinne, "MP Patty Hajdu Feels 'Back Home' as Minister of Health," *TBnewswatch*, November 21, 2019.

50 Thunder Bay Drug Strategy Steering Committee, *Roadmap for Change: Towards a Safe and Healthy Community* (City of Thunder Bay, March 2011).

51 Patricia Hajdu, "Key Factors Contributing to Political Adoption of Municipal Drug Strategies: A Review of Three Canadian Cities" (MPA project, University of Victoria, 2015).

52 Jordan Press, "Legalizing Hard Drugs Not a 'Panacea' to Opioids Crisis, Trudeau Says," *Globe and Mail*, December 19, 2019.

53 BC Human Rights Tribunal, "BCHR Complaint M. Johnson," November 21, 2020, www.heiltsuknation.ca/wp-content/uploads/2020/11/2020-11-22-BCHR-Complaint-M.-Johnson-FINAL-combined.pdf.

54 Hina Alam, "Federal Health Minister Says Too Early for Broad Drug Decriminalization," *Victoria News*, January 17, 2020.

55 Jen St. Denis, "With Nearly Half of City Residents Losing Work, Vancouver Could Face Insolvency: Mayor," *CTV News Vancouver*, April 12, 2020.

56 Special Purpose Committee on the Decriminalization of Illicit Drugs, *Decriminalization for Simple Possession of Illicit Drugs: Exploring Impacts of Public Safety and*

Policing—Findings and Recommendations Report
(Canadian Association of Chiefs of Police, July 2020).

57 Bethany Lindsay, "Seven Years into Crisis, Politicians
Still Struggle to See Drug-Users as People, Dr. Bonnie
Henry Says," *CBC News*, March 7, 2023.

58 "Oregon Measure 110, Drug Decriminalization and
Addiction Treatment Initiative (2020)," *Ballotpedia*,
November 3, 2020.

59 Enshrined in law in California, Oregon and some other
US states, as well as in British Columbia, initiative
processes allow the public to gather signatures on
petitions. If a certain number of signatures is collected
and verified, jurisdictions with initiative laws must
hold a binding public vote (called a referendum) or a
non-binding one (called a plebiscite) as to whether to
proceed with the action for which the petitioners are
calling.

60 Government of Canada, "Controlled Drugs and
Substances Act."

61 Statistics Canada, "Table 8: Police-Reported Crime for
Selected Drug Offences, by Province or Territory, 2021"
and "Table 9: Police-Reported Crime for Selected Drug
Offences, Canada, 2020 and 2021."

62 Ministry of Public Safety and Solicitor General, *Policing and Security Branch, British Columbia Regional District Crime Trends*, 2012–2021 (November 2022).

63 City of Vancouver, *Request for an Exemption from the Controlled Drugs and Substances Act (CDSA) Pursuant to Section 56(1) That Would Decriminalize Personal Possession of Illicit Substances within the City of Vancouver: Final Submission to Health Canada* (May 28, 2021), vancouver.ca/files/cov/request-for-exemption-from-controlled-drugs-and-substances-act.pdf.

64 John Horgan, Mandate letter to Minister Sheila Malcomson, November 26, 2020, news.gov.bc.ca/files/MMHA-Malcolmson-mandate.pdf.

65 Katie DeRosa and Tiffany Crawford, "B.C. Asks Ottawa to Decriminalize Drug Possession After Record Year for Overdose Deaths," *Vancouver Sun*, February 11, 2021.

66 City of Vancouver, *Preliminary Submission to Health Canada: Exemption Request* (March 1, 2021), vancouver.ca/files/cov/cdsa-preliminary-exemption-request.pdf.

67 Vancouver Area Network of Drug Users, "The 'Vancouver Model' of Decriminalization Will Set a Dangerous Precedent for Drug Users Across Canada," *The Mainlander*, May 3, 2021.

68 Vancouver Area Network of Drug Users (@VANDUpeople), "VANDU resigns from the @CityofVancouver Decriminalization Working Group," Twitter, May 10, 2021.

69 Health Canada Expert Task Force on Substance Use, *Report 1: Recommendations on Alternatives to Criminal Penalties for Simple Possession of Controlled Substances* (Health Canada, May 6, 2021).

70 Cindy E. Harnett, "Green MLA Speaks Out on Drug Use, Urges Government to Move Faster on Opioid Crisis," *Vancouver Sun*, October 23, 2021.

71 Ministry of Mental Health and Addictions, *Decriminalization in BC: S.56(1) Exemption* (Government of British Columbia, October 2021), news. gov.bc.ca/files/DecrimSubmission.pdf.

72 Ministry of Mental Health and Addictions, *Decriminalization.*

73 Sozan Savehilaghi, "BC's Decriminalization Plan Doesn't Go Far Enough," *Pivot*, November 1, 2021.

74 Dirk Meissner, "B.C. Applies to Remove Criminal Penalties for Possession of Small Amounts of Drugs," *City News*, November 2, 2021.

75 Ordinarily, private member's bills are not a big deal, as they are mostly performative in nature. Members of Parliament all have the right to table as many bills as they wish for consideration by the House of Commons. While government bills come to the House of Commons floor for debate whenever the government chooses, private member's bills are debated only if an MP is lucky enough to win a lottery draw held at the beginning of the first session of every Parliament. This procedure involves the names of all eligible members being placed in a random draw to establish the order in which private members' business will be considered, with each member eligible to put forward only one bill or motion for debate if their number comes up. It would be rare for a hundred private member's bills to be debated in a majority Parliament, with under thirty passing into law, almost all sponsored by members on the government side of the House, as opposition members rarely succeed in securing the votes needed to pass their bill. However, it is much more possible for private member's bills to pass in a minority Parliament, if, for example, an opposition MP can convince government backbenchers or members from other opposition parties to vote in the affirmative.

76 Erika Ibrahim, "Health Canada Mulling B.C.'s Drug Decriminalization Request but with Lower Threshold: Minister," *Global News*, April 6, 2022.

77 Cable Public Affairs Channel (@cpac), "Federal Govt Grants B.C. Exemption to Decriminalize Personal Drug Possession—May 31, 2022," Cable Public Affairs Channel, May 31, 2022 (streamed announcement, YouTube, 1:08:08).

78 Bethany Lindsay, "B.C. Decriminalization Plan Won't Do Much to Stop Toxic Deaths, Says Chief Coroner," *CBC News*, May 31, 2022.

79 Canadian Drug Policy Coalition, "'We Need Decriminalization for All:' Drug Policy and Human Rights Organizations Say Model in British Columbia Leaves Many Behind" (news release, June 1, 2022).

80 Pierre Poilievre (@PierrePoilievre), Twitter, May 31, 2022.

81 Dan Fumano, "The Fight For and Against Affordable Rental Housing in Vancouver," *Vancouver Sun*, April 5, 2019.

82 Jason Proctor, "Thomus Donaghy Saved Many Lives from Overdoses. His Killer Wants to Ensure His Life 'Wasn't for Nothing,'" *CBC News*, December 14, 2021.

83 If all this was not enough, the *Globe and Mail* reported in March 2023 that China's Vancouver consulate interfered in the 2022 municipal election and worked to secure my defeat. The *Globe* reported, "China's

diplomatic mission in Vancouver has actively interfered in the city's politics, using proxies in diaspora community organizations and grooming politicians to run in last fall's municipal election, according to Canada's spy agency." (Robert Fife, Steven Chase and Nathan Vanderklippe, "China's Vancouver Consulate Interfered in 2022 Municipal Election According to CSIS," *Globe and Mail*, March 16, 2023.)

84 Bethany Lindsay, "Reports of Assault, Verbal Abuse as Thousands Protest Vaccine Passports Outside Hospitals across B.C.," *CBC News*, September 1, 2021.

85 Sarah Anderson, "Ted Cruz Takes Shots at Vancouver Mayor Kennedy Stewart on Twitter," *Daily Hive News*, February 5, 2022.

86 For more on PPN, see Dan Fumano, "Have Big-Money, U.S.-Style Politics come to B.C.?," *Vancouver Sun*, August 3, 2022; Press Progress, "PPN: Change Starts Locally" (photograph, 2022), pressprogress.ca/wp-content/uploads/2022/10/thumb-2022-10-07.png.

87 Justin McElroy, "Vancouver Mayor Kennedy Stewart Calls for Province to Review Policing across B.C.," *CBC News*, June 11, 2020.

88 Ruth Montgomery et al., *Vancouver Police Board Street Check Review* (Vancouver Police Board, December 17, 2019).

89 Mike Howell, "Vancouver NPA Accuses Mayor of 'Hate Speech' in Court Action," *Business Intelligence for BC*, February 4, 2021.

90 Sarah Grochowski, "Aaron Gunn Tossed from B.C. Liberal Leadership Race over 'Diversity Concerns,'" *Times Colonist*, October 22, 2021.

91 Bob Mackin, "Ken Sim's ex-Chief of Staff Opens Up About ABC Election Strategy," *Business Intelligence for BC*, April 27, 2023.

92 Mike Howell, "Election 2022: Why Ken Sim Wants to Be Mayor of Vancouver," *Vancouver Is Awesome*, September 7, 2022.

93 Office of the Federal Housing Advocate (@HousingLogement), "I am concerned by reports that @CityofVancouver and @VancouverPD are dismantling the homeless encampment on Hastings Street in Vancouver," Twitter, April 5, 2023.

94 BBC Federation of Labour, "BCFED Condemns Mayor Sim's 'Callous, Dehumanizing,' DTES Tactics," (*BCFED*, news release, April 12, 2023).

95 Shawn Ayers and Hana Mae Nassar, "VANDU Arts, Culture Grant Pulled Due to 'Misuse' of Prior Funds: City of Vancouver," *City News*, January 18, 2023.

96 Dan Fumano, "Non-Profits Seeking Funds Must Be 'Respectful,' Vancouver Council Says," *Vancouver Sun*, March 28, 2023.

97 Abigail Turner, "Councillor Says Yaletown Overdose Prevention Site Will Be Moved, Citing 'Safety Issues,'" *CTV News Vancouver*, April 27, 2023.

98 Health Canada, "Table 15. Illegal Drug Use (Past 12-Month and Lifetime), by Age Group and Sex, 2019," (Canadian Alcohol and Drugs Survey [CADS] 2019) www.canada.ca/en/health-canada/services/canadian-alcohol-drugs-survey/2019-summary/detailed-tables.html#t15.

99 Jordan Omstead, "Toronto Wants to Expand Drug Decriminalization to Cover All Ages and Substances," *CBC News*, March 24, 2023.

100 Dan Reist, *Methadone Maintenance Treatment in British Columbia, 1996–2008: Analysis and Recommendations* (Ministry of Healthy Living and Sport, May 2010); Tom Blackwell, "Critics Question Methadone Usage as Patient Numbers Soar in Canada," *National Post*, March 15, 2016.

101 Moira Wyton, "'I Want Them to Break Up with Their Drug Dealer,'" *The Tyee*, April 11, 2022.

102 Darcy Hango and Sébastien LaRochelle-Côté, *Association between the Frequency of Cannabis Use and Selected Social Indicators* (Statistics Canada, May 3, 2018).

103 Akshay Kulkarni, "Vancouver Votes to Support Application That Would Create Safe Drug 'Compassion Clubs,'" *CBC News*, October 7, 2021.

ACKNOWLEDGEMENTS

I AM GRATEFUL TO THOSE WHO HAVE HELPED MAKE THIS BOOK possible; my apologies to those unintentionally omitted. I first want to thank my soulmate and confidante Jeanette for everything always, and Fergus for keeping my feet warm while I typed this book. I am so grateful to my brother Evan, sister Julia and mother Cathy for their unending love. Thank you, Ray Havelock, for sharing Susan's story, and Siobhan for your generosity of spirit. I've learned so much about front-line nursing from Mairead Ashe and cherish her and Brad's friendship. Thanks to Tommy and Margie Ashe for making me feel so much at home every time I visit them in Port Coquitlam. Special thanks to Professor Paddy Smith from Simon Fraser University for his guidance and encouraging my love of cities.

I have so many people to thank for my fulfilling political career, but want to single out my mayor's office team—Neil, Anita, Alvin, Lauren, Laurie, Alex, Simka and Akeena—for their effort to secure decriminalization and everything else we accomplished, as well as Mark Hosak and the 2018 and 2022 campaign teams for all their work. Special thanks to Neil Monckton for sticking with me through thick and thin, and to Kera and Doug McArthur and Fred and Maggie for supporting Neil's important political adventures.

No one knows more about what we need to do to end the war on drug users than the intrepid Karen Ward, and thanks to Dean Wilson for all he has done for Vancouver. Thanks to Sarah Blyth for her unparalleled overdose prevention site and other work, and to Trey Helten for his dedication to saving lives. Thanks to Garth Mullins, Fiona York, Jean Swanson, the late Chrissy Brett and other community leaders for constantly pushing us to do better. And thanks to Libby Davies from all of us for spending a lifetime championing those living in the Downtown Eastside.

Thanks to Dr. Patricia Daly, chief medical health officer for Vancouver Coastal Health, for being a rock through the two worst health crises the city has ever faced, and to Dr. Mark Tyndall and Dr. Christy Sutherland for pushing the treatment envelope and for the care they show to their patients and colleagues. Professor Kora DeBeck deserves special mention for her valuable academic work and important contributions to the Vancouver and British Columbia exemption application.

Thanks to the City of Vancouver's leadership team, including city manager Paul Mochrie and deputy city managers Karen Levitt and Armin Amrolia, for their incredible professionalism, competence and dedication. The same to the wonderful staff of the Arts, Culture, and Community Services Department, who supported the Mayor's Overdose Emergency Task Force and decriminalization effort, including General Manager Sandra Singh, Managing Director of Social Policy Mary Clare Zak, and Community Action Team Coordinator Alycia Fridkin, and the seventy members of the CAT advisory team. I appreciate Vancouver chief constable Adam Palmer's efforts to lead police chiefs across the country to advocate for drug decriminalization. I also want to thank Vancouver Fire and Rescue Services Chief Karen Fry and the firefighters who have done so much to help during this terrible time.

At the federal level, I wish to thank Prime Minister Justin Trudeau for being so generous with his time during my time as mayor and doing more to support municipalities than any of his predecessors. I also want to thank many of the Liberal cabinet members, especially the Honourable Patty Hajdu for pushing open the decriminalization window, and the Honourable Dr. Carolyn Bennett for pulling us all through. Thanks to Ahmed Hussen for all the housing funding, especially through the pandemic, and to Nathaniel Erskine-Smith for the courage to lead on this issue in the Liberal Party. On Team Orange, thank you to Jagmeet Singh for encouraging the NDP to embrace decriminalization (and for getting dental care!) and to MP Gord Johns for going to the wall for this issue.

One part of my job as mayor that I most cherished was working with Musqueam Band Chief Wayne Sparrow, Squamish Council Chair Khelsilem and Tsleil-Waututh Nation Chief Jen Thomas. I am so grateful for what I have learned from these leaders and their councils, and for their early support for decriminalizing drugs on their traditional, unceded, ancestral territories. Urban Indigenous leaders were also very generous with their time and support, especially members of the Metro Vancouver Aboriginal Executive Council.

Finally, thanks to all at Harbour Publishing, especially publisher Anna Comfort O'Keeffe, publicist Fleur Matthewson and editor Brian Lynch.

APPENDIX

From: ███████████████████████████████

Sent: Wednesday, September 21, 2022 9:00 AM

To: Stewart, K ████████████████████████████████
██
██

Cc: ██
██
██
████████████████████

Subject: Weekly overdose data for September 12-September 18

Hi all,

Here is this week's overdose report. VPD attended **11 overdose-suspected deaths** last week, bringing our year-to-date estimate to at least **370 people in the City of Vancouver** who have died in 2022 from an overdose.

<u>Significant Data: September 12 - September 18</u>

- VPD reporting **11 OD deaths, 1 above last week** (3 above the 2021 estimated weekly average)
  - No deaths at City-owned properties

- VFRS reporting **77 OD calls, 26 fewer than last week**
  (72 below the 2021 weekly average)
    - Down 25% from last week
    - No fire calls at City-owned properties

2022 Year-to-date Data

- Estimated **370+ overdose deaths** in the City of Vancouver in 2022
  to date
- **2,531+** deaths in Vancouver since Public Health Emergency
  declared in April 2016
    - Latest BC Coroners Service Report was released on
      September 15, with data through end of July 2022
    - VPD data has been used to estimate the number of deaths in
      August and September 2022
- VFRS reported OD calls:
- Year-to-date Average: 152

2021 Summary Data

- **533 overdose deaths** in the City of Vancouver in 2021
  *Reported by the BC Coroners Service in August 2022
- VFRS reported OD calls: 2021 Average: 148 calls/week

2020 Summary Data

- **422 overdose deaths** in the City of Vancouver in 2020
  *Reported by the BC Coroners Service in August 2022
- VFRS reported OD calls: 2020 Average: 79 calls/week

INDEX

of drugs, 4, 57, 60, 76,
83, 158–59
See also cocaine, heroin
Liberal Party, 45, 47, 50–54,
61, 83–84, 86, 107,
127–28
convention delegates,
45
Livingston, Ann, 38–39

McArthur, Doug, 65
MacPherson, Donald, 40, 85
Malcolmson, Sheila, 107, 115,
127, 131
May, Elizabeth, 64
Mayor's Overdose
Emergency Task
Force, 71
methadone, 157
Miller, David, 89
Monckton, Neil, 69, 92
Mulcair, Thomas, 48–52, 54,
55–56
Musqueam Indian Band
(xʷməθkʷəy̓əm), 9
reserve lands, 107

naloxone, 71, 73
National Institute of Mental
Health, 2

needle exchange program,
4, 22, 35–36, 42
New Democratic Party
(NDP), 46, 49–50,
54, 86
federal government, 61,
97–98
provincial government,
36
NIMBY ("not in my
backyard"), 135,
141–42
Non-Partisan Association
(NPA), 20, 35, 39–41,
69, 71–72, 141–42
councillors, 69, 90, 101
North American Free
Trade Agreement
(1988), 34

opioid agonist therapy
(OAT), 157
opioids crisis, 10, 96
Opium Act, 58
overdose
crisis, 1–2, 74, 94–96, 154
statistics, 10–11, **12**,
25–**26**–**27**, 37–38, 42
prevention, 17

ABOUT THE AUTHOR

Kennedy Stewart is a politician, educator, author and co-editor of *Turning Parliament Inside Out: Practical Ideas for Reforming Canada's Democracy* (Douglas & McIntyre, 2017). After serving as mayor of Vancouver for four years he is now back teaching at Simon Fraser University's School of Public Policy. He rents in Vancouver, BC, with his wife, Dr. Jeanette Ashe, and dog Fergus.